Sovereign Nations
or
Reservations?

An Economic History
of American Indians

Toll Collectors by Charles M. Russell (1913) is in the Mackay
Collection and is reprinted with permission of the Montana
Historical Society, Helena, Montana

Sovereign Nations
or
Reservations?

An Economic History
of American Indians

Terry L. Anderson

LCCC LIBRARY
PACIFIC RESEARCH INSTITUTE FOR PUBLIC POLICY
SAN FRANCISCO, CA

ISBN 0-936488-81-6

Printed in the United States of America
10   9   8   7   6   5   4   3   2   1

PACIFIC RESEARCH INSTITUTE FOR PUBLIC POLICY
755 Sansome Street, Suite 450
San Francisco, CA 94111
(415) 989-0833

Distributed to the trade by National Book Network, Lanham, MD.

Library of Congress Cataloging-in-Publication Data
Anderson, Terry Lee [date]
    Sovereign nations or reservations? : an economic history of American Indians / Terry L. Anderson
        p.   cm.
    Includes bibliographical references (p.   ) and index.
    ISBN 0-036488-81-6
    1. Indians of North America—Economic conditions. 2. Indians of North America—Great Plains—Economic conditions.
E98.E2A53   1995
330.973′008997—dc20   94-43439
                                                                                             CIP

Cover Design: *Judith Haig*
Index: *Shirley Kessel, Primary Sources Research*
Printing and Binding: *Data Reproductions Corporation*

DEDICATION

Dedicated to my tribe,
Janet, Sarah, and Peter

CONTENTS

F O R E W O R D

The collapse of centralized state planning in the Commu-
nist world and the discrediting of socialism in the non-Commu-
nist world have brought about a real revolution in our
understanding of first and second world societies. Is it not
appropriate that our understanding of third and fourth world
societies should share this revolution? This is what Terry L.
Anderson has done in this extraordinary book *Sovereign Nations or Reservations?* Anderson looks at the interaction of
Indians and whites not in terms of moral absolutes or romantic
images but in terms of how property rights were defined,
valued, transferred, or defended by both sides from initial
contact to the present day. "*Homo economicus,*" he asserts, "was
alive and well in the pre-European Indian culture" as well as
in that of the white settlers. Indian respect (or disrespect) for
nature is seen as a rational utilitarian response to economic
and cultural imperatives. Anderson argues that Indian economic well-being is determined not by an abundance of resources, physical or human, but by institutional environments
that stimulate productive use of what resources do exist. In the
wake of the evidence provided by the Pacific Rim economies of
Japan, Korea, Hong Kong, and Singapore, we can no longer
ignore such conclusions. In the case of Native American socie-

ties, Anderson draws from the contrasting evidence of the economic success of different tribes, for example, the Crow Indians in comparison with the Blackfeet. Nor can we ignore Anderson's interpretation of the effects of the General Allotment Act of 1887 and the Indian Reorganization Act of 1934, both legislative enactments, says Anderson, "limited the ability of individual Indians and tribes to manage their resources and reduced the role of informal institutions in the governance structure." Anderson argues that Indians who received land in fee simple after the breakup of tribal lands were more productive than those individuals whose land was encumbered by the continuing "trust" relationship with the federal government, and even more productive than the land retained under tribal control under a similar trust relationship. The Indian Reorganization Act, by ignoring some of the individualistic features of many Indian tribes in favor of enhancing the sovereign authority of tribal governments, created a system that worked if the constitutional system adopted fit local customs. But too often this resulted in a parody of democratic government when the system failed to take into account the possibility of abuse by those chosen to administer it (variously "rent seekers" or "free riders" in the economic equation).

Anderson modestly (and appropriately in my mind, since not all scholars are prepared to accept his analysis) concludes not with definitive policy prescriptions in the manner of so many past "Friends of the Indian" but with a statement of what can be learned from Indian history and policy by applying the public choice economic interpretation he has brought to the study of Indian history. Though anthropologists and historians are normally ignorant of, or disinclined to consider, economic theory in their study of the American Indian, Anderson's provocative conclusions provide a challenge that no student of Indian-white relations can ignore. Underlying his thesis is a profound confidence in the ability of individual Indians to compete successfully if bound neither by restrictive bureaucratic regulations nor, in the case of tribal officials subsidized by a paternalistic government, lured into nonproductive political activities designed to transfer wealth rather than to create it.

Wilcomb E. Washburn
Smithsonian Institution

P R E F A C E

My interest in Indian property rights began in 1976 when I took a Swiss family to visit a Montana Indian reservation. Because they had never visited a reservation and had a romantic European image of the American Indian, I was trying to prepare them for the poverty, substandard housing, and other problems typically found on reservations. As we approached the home of the Indian family we were going to visit, however, it was clear that my rendition of reservation life did not fit this family. Set against a backdrop of spectacular Montana mountains was a beautiful home, well-kept yard, and productive fields. The Swiss visitors must have been skeptical of my knowledge of American Indians and well they should have been. That knowledge came from my time as a youth spent on a cattle ranch near the Blackfeet reservation in Montana. At the time, I knew almost nothing of the political and legal environments in which Indian economies operated.

After getting acquainted with the Indian we were visiting, I could not resist asking if he would explain what appeared to be an atypical reservation lifestyle. Why was this ranch so productive, why was the house so well kept, and why was his income so much higher than the average American Indian's? Was my general impression of reservation economies incorrect, or was this particular Indian family doing better than average? In response to my questions, he gave me a rather puzzled look and answered matter-of-factly, "I own this place." When asked if we were on the reservation, he answered "Yes" and proceeded to explain that there was private land mixed with Indian land on most reservations. That was my first inkling of the complexity of Indian land tenure and the legal environment in which resource management decisions on reservations are made.

Immediately I thought that it would be interesting to examine whether there was any relationship between the extent of private ownership on reservations and the level of reservation incomes. My economic studies of property rights led me to hypothesize that more private ownership, all else being equal, would lead to higher incomes because private owners of land have more incentive to be productive. When I returned to the university, my first stop was the library, where I searched for data on Indian incomes and reservation ownership patterns. Unfortunately, the search turned up a dearth of data; nearly a dozen years lapsed before I returned to the research agenda.

The rekindling of my interest in Indian economies came from Chip Mellor, then president of Pacific Research Institute in San Francisco. Chip knew of my research dealing with property rights on the Anglo-American frontier and called to see whether I had studied American Indian issues. In fact, he asked whether I was interested in writing a book on the subject. After several weeks of consideration and persistent encouragement from Chip, I said "Yes." Unfortunately, it took eight years for the manuscript to take shape, mostly because I had so far to climb on the learning curve.

The long gestation period, however, has led to a better product. Given the dearth of data, time allowed me to explore some innovative ways to examine the empirical relationship between economic activity on reservations and their institutional environment. In the process, I learned a great deal from other scholars, especially Dean Lueck and Fred McChesney, and other authors who contributed to a book I edited titled *Property Rights and Indian Economies (1992)*.

In the research process, I discovered Charlie Russell's

painting *Toll Collectors* (frontispiece) and John Clymer's *The Cattle Drive.** Each painting depicts cattle drive bosses followed by their herds being confronted by Indians. In *The Cattle Drive,* three Indians signal for the trail boss to stop, indicating that the herd is about to encroach on Indian territory. In *Toll Collectors,* an Indian brave holds up two fingers while his companions cut two steers from the herd. The "transaction" between the trail boss and the Indians suggests that Indians had a claim on the territory and that they were able to enforce that claim. Moreover, the trail boss was "willing" to allow the Indians to take cattle from the herd in exchange for passage through the territory.

These paintings reveal several important insights regarding the history of Indian-white relations as they are described in this book. Evident in the paintings is the fact that Indian-white relations were not always violent, with whites taking land from the Indians. Especially during the first half of the nineteenth century, Indians had the might to control access to certain territories.

Because the medium of these paintings is static, however, it leaves much about the details of the transaction to the imagination and raises several questions. Who is the small band of Indians to whom the toll is being paid? Are they highway robbers extorting value from the trail boss who knows he is outnumbered and will lose more if he resists? Or are they acting as agents, the police force, for a larger sovereign political unit? What rights are they conveying to the trail boss? Is it simply a right of safe passage, and if so, for how far? Are they leasing grass on land they as individuals or as a collective own? What determines the amount of the toll? If the Indians have the stronger military force, why don't they simply take the entire herd? Does the willingness of the Indians to engage in trade mean that markets were not inimical to their culture? If *Toll Collectors* suggests a recognition of Indian property rights and a willingness to trade, what changed during the nineteenth century to allow whites to take land they wanted through force?

---

* The former is found in the Montana Historical Society, Helena, Montana, and the latter in the Buffalo Bill Historical Center, Cody, Wyoming.

These questions are the subject of the first four chapters of the book. Chapter 1 considers the general relationship between property rights, culture, and economic activity broadly defined. Relying heavily on insights of Nobel laureate Douglass C. North, this chapter defines institutions as the term is used here, explores the determinants of institutional change for Indians from pre-Columbian times to the present, and explains the relationship between American Indian institutions and economic performance. Chapter 2 examines Indian law prior to European contact and illustrates its decentralized nature. Generally, Indians had little experience with strong tribal leadership except in warfare, relying more on small groups, clans, and families for social control.

Perhaps the most important lesson from this book is that American Indian institutions were far from static but evolved in response to environmental and market conditions. As discussed in Chapter 3, Indians readily adapted their institutions to meet changing economic and environmental conditions even before contact with Europeans. Where appropriate, they established private ownership. By necessity, Indian society was dynamic rather than static. Contact with whites accelerated that evolutionary process by significantly lowering transportation costs with the introduction of the horse and by introducing Indians to expanded trade opportunities. The response of Indian institutions to these changes is the subject of Chapter 4.

Institutional change amongst American Indians took on a very different flavor when it was dictated by the bureaucracy in Washington, D.C. The sad story of bureaucracy versus the Indians begins with the Indian Wars in the latter half of the nineteenth century. Following the Civil War, the large standing army justified its existence by fighting Indians on the frontier, the subject of Chapter 5. Following relegation to reservations, U.S. land policy further entrenched the federal bureaucracy in Indian affairs. Federal policy tried to force individual ownership of small land parcels on Indians and later placed Indian lands permanently under the trusteeship of the Bureau of Indian Affairs. This resulting mosaic of land tenure today thwarts productivity on reservations, as the data in Chapter 6 confirm.

The next sad episode in Indian history began when the

Indian Reorganization Act of 1934 tried to establish constitutional governments for each tribe. While the idea of limiting the authority of tribal government and leaders was nothing new to American Indians, the "one size fits all" democratic constitutions proposed for tribes were not always consistent with tribal traditions. Chapter 7 argues that top down dictation of institutions has resulted in inappropriate institutions and has been primarily responsible for the plight of American Indians.

Somewhere between wardship and sovereignty lies the hope for self-determination. American Indians have a history of establishing institutions consistent with their cultures and traditions and with their environment. Ignoring this tradition that often relied on individual and family property rights leaves out part of their rich cultural heritage. Similarly, sovereignty does not mean that Indian economies will prosper if tribal governments are given unlimited powers. Chapter 8 summarizes the lessons we can learn from the institutional history of American Indians.

Ever since the white man's government began dictating Indian institutions through reservation policies such as the Dawes Act (1887) or the Indian Reorganization Act (1934), the cultural heritage of Indians has been ignored. Yet that heritage is rich with examples of "getting the incentives right." Survival and even prosperity, especially in the often harsh, arid environments where the Plains Indians lived, required that they adopt rules for governing their lives that rewarded productive behavior. Even in the Northwest where nature's bounty made life easier, scarce time and capital had to be allocated among competing ends if productivity was to occur. It was not some mystic reverence for nature that encouraged resource stewardship but formal and informal rules (what economists call property rights) that forced individuals and small groups to confront the costs and benefits of their actions. Rather than promulgating myths that societies can solve their economic and social problems only by consciously choosing to revere and respect plant and animal communities, we should learn from American Indians that it is the institutional environment that matters most. While the physical environment will certainly impose constraints, the absence of an institutional environment that gets the incentives right will overpower reverence and ideology.

If Indians are to enjoy true self-determination, they will have to delve into their institutional heritage and begin building sovereignty from the bottom up. This heritage reveals how adaptable Indians have been and how important formal and informal rules have been in their survival and prosperity.

I want to say a few words about my choice to describe the subjects of this study as American Indians instead of Native Americans. I chose the former because it more accurately describes the indigenous population of North America. I too am a native American, but I am not an Indian; my ancestors migrated to this continent just as did theirs. I was born here and have no homeland to which I can or should return. Often the term *Native American* is used to imply that Indians were here first and therefore have superior rights. Without a doubt, they did have some rights, especially to land, that derived from a Lockean notion of "first in time, first in right," and for a while those rights were recognized by the European immigrants. However, whether by negotiation or force, Americans—Indians and non-Indians alike—have come to the distribution of land we have today. Calls to revisit the fairness of the results are justified, but we cannot escape the fact that all of today's native Americans and immigrants have a legitimate right to live in the sovereign nation we call the United States. If we are to live together peacefully and prosperously, our task is to discover and develop stable institutions that encourage cooperation rather than confrontation.

Whatever the injustices of the past, the message of this book is that clear and stable rules for individuals voluntarily interacting with one another provide the best hope for freedom and responsibility for all Americans, Indians and non-Indians alike. American Indians understood the importance of individual freedom and responsibility prior to their contact with Anglo-American government; unfortunately, the institutions that promoted this were eroded as the federal government treated Indians as wards of the state. All Americans can benefit from reconsidering the causes and impacts of the erosion of individual rights that has accompanied this policy.

Acknowledgments

No project like this would be possible without the cooperation of many others. To Chip Mellor who planted the seed for the project, thanks for your confidence, patience, and your friendship. To the scholars from whom I have learned so much, Dan Benjamin, Bruce Benson, Leonard Carlson, Stephen Cornell, Bill Dennis, David Haddock, P. J. Hill, Joseph Kalt, Bob Nelson, Jennifer Roback, and Rick Stroup, to mention a few, please accept my apologies for not thanking you enough and for the mistakes that have not been corrected. To Dean Lueck and Fred McChesney, my coauthors on two papers dealing with Indian land tenure and the political economy of the Indian Wars, respectively, thanks for teaching me so much about data analysis, institutions, and Indian history. To the students, especially Claire Morgan, Angela Huschka, and Steven LaCombe, who helped with the research, thanks for making my life easier. To the foundations such as the M. J. Murdock Charitable Trust, the Sarah Scaife Foundation, the Earhart Foundation, and the Charles Redd Foundation, which provided financial support for the research, thanks for your willingness to invest. To the people at the Political Economy Research Center who provided research and clerical support to say nothing of their moral support, thanks for being like family. Finally, to my wife Janet, daughter Sarah, and son Peter who put up with my moods, didn't disturb me when I was writing in the early morning hours, and listened unendingly to my dinner-table lectures on Indian history, thanks for your love and support at all times. I hope you all accept this book as a small token of my appreciation.

CHAPTER 1

Culture, Property Rights, and Paradigms

Despite abundant natural resources of land, timber, wildlife, and energy, Indian reservations remain among the most impoverished areas in the United States. According to 1990 census data, 22 percent of Indian households on reservations had incomes of less than $5000 per year compared with 6 percent for the overall U.S. population. At the other end of the income distribution, only 8 percent of reservation households had incomes greater than $35,000 compared with 18 percent for the nation as a whole.[1] In 1990, 31 percent of Indian households received public assistance income, and 23 percent were below the poverty line (U.S. Bureau of the Census, 1990, p. 77). Unemployment rates are also extremely high and rising on reservations. Between 1979 and 1989 the unemployment rate on reservations rose from 27 percent to 40 percent while the unemployment rate for the nation as a whole hovered between 5 and 7 percent.

The poor economic performance of reservations has been attributed to a number of variables, ranging from the lack of physical and human capital to cultural differences between Indians and western society. Cornell and Kalt (1992a) categorize the lack of growth under four main explanations:

▶ "those that attribute underdevelopment to powerlessness, dependency, and expropriation" (p. 225);

▶ "those that treat differential outcomes as factorial in economic terms" (p. 225);

▶ "those that cite intrinsic aspects of Indian societies, usually indigenous culture or tribal social organization" (p. 226); and

▶ "those that blame persistent poverty on the absence of effective governing institutions" (p. 227).

The first of these explanations focuses on past expropriation of resources and on the current Indian dependence on the federal government for income. According to this theory, Indian economies will only prosper "as tribes are freed from paternalistic controls and exploitative economic relations with the larger society" (Cornell & Kalt, 1992a, 225). The second explanation is more in keeping with traditional development economics in that it focuses on endowments of human and physical capital and on natural resources. But, as with international comparisons of economic performance, these endowments tend to be neither necessary nor sufficient conditions for growth. As Cornell and Kalt note: "The Crows and the White Mountain Apaches are resource-rich, but the wealthier tribe in resource terms [the Crows] is the poorer tribe by almost every measure of performance" (1992a, p. 226).

The third explanation, because the "Indians are different," seems pervasive, but it deserves critical attention. For much of this century, Indian policy began with the premise that "Indian economic development can proceed only as the process of acculturation allows" (U.S. Bureau of Indian Affairs, 1969, p. 333). More recently, "acculturation" has fallen by the wayside and has been replaced with the idea that no culture is dominant and that no culture is better than another. As Robert Royal puts it, multiculturalism "suggests a substantive pluralism, a quintessentially modern American culture of cultures in which no voice predominates—save the voice that says that no voice shall predominate" (1992, p. 3).

At the same time, however, the voice that says no culture shall predominate criticizes the European degradation of pristine indigenous cultures. Especially with the quincentenary of

Columbus' arrival in the New World, the Anglo-European Judeo-Christian cultural intrusion onto the western side of the Atlantic is seen as a strike against multiculturalism and a step backward on the path of cultural advancement.[2] This step backward is especially evident in the alleged change in man's relationship with nature. The argument is that western culture, which encourages excessive resource consumption, is "unsustainable" and that individuals indoctrinated by this culture must voluntarily change their behavior or be forced to change by impending resource shortages. Indigenous populations inhabiting the North American, African, and Australian continents prior to colonization by Europeans are put forth as examples of environmentally sensitive cultures who understood "sustainable" behavior.

There can be no doubt that cultural differences existed and continue to exist among the indigenous populations and between these people and the European immigrants who crossed the Atlantic. American Indians often worshiped the sun, the earth, and the animals upon which their subsistence depended. Accordingly, primitive religions and their rituals are said to have taught Indians to live in harmony with their natural environment. Modern multicultural scholars contend that Indians were not corrupted by the self-interest of capitalism. Hence, they contend that "there is a deep perception in the Indian world that the over-all thinking of the 'White Man' lacks roots, is not well-squared with the laws of nature and the universe. There is a belief that this has been the root of untold misery for native peoples" (Barreiro, 1988, p. vii). Therefore, what the Indian has to offer western society is a set of ideals and values for proper social and environmental living according to Indian's *communitas,* which includes sharing power and property equally (see Barreiro, 1988, pp. vii–xi). Traditions like the potlatch, wherein Indians of the Pacific Northwest shared their wealth with fellow members of their clans and tribes, and Plains Indians sharing buffalo meat after a hunt are offered as examples of *communitas.*

But it is difficult to find a correlation between the different Indian cultures and the performance of Indian economies. After reviewing several tribal differences, Cornell and Kalt conclude that "evidence suggests that indigenous culture, in and of itself, is not the obstacle to development that it is often portrayed to be. It may shape political and economic development in important ways . . . but it is probably not necessary to stop being tribal or 'traditional' to develop economically" (1992a, p. 227). Nonetheless, most students of American Indian anthropology, sociology, politics, and law have accepted the cultural differences explanation and shun the analytical framework of economics with its emphasis on rational self-interest. If culture explains human action, little room is left for the egocentric individual who maximizes wealth or well-being subject to constraints imposed by the physical and institutional environment.

Posner notes that the debate over "the applicability of the economic model of human behavior to primitive man" is left "sterile" because the "contending groups share an excessively narrow view of what is economic" (1980, pp. 1–2). This narrow view has centered mostly on explicit market transactions involving goods and services traded at their market prices, with "formalists" arguing that primitive societies had formal markets and "substantivists" arguing that such markets were foreign to primitive societies.[3] Hence, debate over the applicability of the economic model has perforce focused mainly on formal market transactions.

This book goes beyond the formalist view and applies economics in a broader perspective. For example, the economic law of demand, which states that individuals faced with higher prices will consume less of the higher priced goods, has important explanatory power outside formal markets. Indian consumption reflected times of abundance when the cost of acquiring food was reduced. When Indians were able to stampede buffalo over cliffs, the abundance of meat allowed them to take only the choicest parts and resulted in piles of rotting carcasses. Hence the distinction between "light butchering," meaning only the best parts of the animal were used when meat was plentiful, and "heavy butchering," meaning full utilization of the animal when scarcity prevailed (Wissler, 1910, pp. 41–42). Certainly culture and ritual were important constraints on Indian behavior, but prices made a difference in everything from their choice of technologies to diets to art. This simple insight is crucial to understanding Indian history.

The final explanation, blaming Indian poverty on ineffective governing institutions, is the focal point of this book. According to this theory, economic stagnation is due to "the lack of institutions capable of effectively regulating and channelling individual and collective behavior" (Cornell & Kalt, 1992a, p. 227). Under the rubric "new institutional economics,"[4] more and more political economists are developing explanations of economic performance that extend the insights of narrower market theories to the area of formal and informal rules that govern societies. The new institutional economist asks what impact "the rules of the game" have on the interaction of individuals including families, clans, tribes, and governments as well as traditional economic markets. They also examine why the institutional environment changes over time. This emerging new institutional economics has integrated the institutional and physical environments into theories that help explain "the rise and decline of nations" (see Olson, 1989).

Recently, a few Indian scholars and government officials have begun to realize the importance of an institutional approach to Indian economic development. Dismissing a lack of human capital as the reason for Indian cattle ranching inefficiency, Trosper concluded that "land tenure or other institutional problems" should be examined as the possible explanation (1978, p. 239). An Interior Department Task Force on Indian Economic Development found that the Bureau of Indian Affairs' trust role over Indian lands "creates complications for efforts to promote the development of the business sector on Indian reservations" (1969, p. 239). Even the below par performance of Alaska's Native corporations has been related to institutional constraints on transferability of shares (Karpoff & Rice, 1989). In an address to the 1992 Reservation Economic Summit, Deputy Commissioner of Indian Affairs David Matheson stated that economic development starts with "the political environment. You have to have an effective tribal government. There should be a well defined and well drawn up tribal constitution. . . . We need to focus first on the political and governmental environment" (Matheson, 1992, pp. 3–4). And in asking "what can tribes do," Cornell and Kalt contend that reservation development will depend on the ability of tribes to find "a match between the formal institutions of governance on the one hand and the culture of the society on the other" (1992b, p. 17).

Finding the correct mix for this institutional environment is essential for understanding Indian economies. By understanding the relationship between the institutional environment and resource constraints, we can develop a clearer picture of why societies progress or digress; why they experience economic growth or stagnation; and why one society comes to dominate another. Just as this integration has furthered our understanding of how and why modern societies grow (see North, Anderson, & Hill, 1983), it can help explain how American Indians were able to adapt to their natural environment and prosper; how they adapted to new technologies and institutions brought by the Europeans; why they have failed to prosper economically in the midst of the richest societies in the world; and how they might restructure their institutions to promote self-determination and economic prosperity. All of this requires an understanding of institutions, institutional change, and economic performance as they apply to American Indians.[5]

Institutions

The institutions important to the organization and development of American Indian societies can be thought of as the rules of the game that determine who is able to derive wealth from the assets available to the society. In this definition, I will focus on two key terms: *rules of the game* and *wealth*. Narrowly conceived, the rules of the game can be taken to mean the legal environment in which economic activities on reservations take place. This would include tribal constitutions, federal laws, and tribal regulations. But formal laws are only one part of the institutional constraints on individual and collective behavior in any society, and in Indian societies formal laws probably play only a minor part. Informal rules, including customs, norms, religious teachings, ideologies, and traditions, can be far more important. These rules are generally unwritten and, rather than being codified by a formal governance structure, evolve over long periods in response to changing physical and human resource constraints at the local level. Even in modern societies such rules and customs can be important, but in societies without written languages informal rules provide the bulk of the institutional framework.

Because the informal rules evolve at a very local level in response to changing economic and environmental conditions, it is likely that the informal rules that survive are those that work. In other words, informal rules or customs that serve little purpose or, worse yet, are counterproductive drop by the wayside or are replaced by new rules (see Alchian, 1950). Given this evolutionary process, it is likely that the informal rules fit the institutional needs of the community and channel resources into productive activities.[6] This should be especially true in subsistence societies where survival depends on efficiency.

Where informal Indian institutions have been replaced by formal rules—constitutions, laws, and regulations—the formal structure has usually come from the federal government.[7] As you will see in later chapters, congressional acts and bureaucratic regulations have played an increasingly important role in determining the plight of reservation economies. Laws such as the Dawes Act (1887) and the Indian Reorganization Act (1934), for example, have limited the ability of individual Indians and tribes to manage their resources and reduced the role of informal institutions in that governance structure. In particular, the mosaic of land tenure on Indian land constrains land management decisions in ways that significantly reduce agricultural productivity. With this top-down imposition of rules, there is less time for evolution and less likelihood that the formal structure will mesh with the informal one. As recent research has shown (see Bates, 1989; Cornell & Kalt, 1992b; North, 1990), the absence of a match between formal and informal institutions is not likely to enhance the prospects for growth.

In considering the impact of institutions on the productivity of a society, it is important to define wealth broadly rather than narrowly referring only to assets that can be measured in monetary terms. Contrary to accepted stereotypes, economists use wealth to mean any human values that contribute to human well-being. So conceived, wealth is necessarily anthropocentric because it depends on human values. This does not mean, however, that animals or plants are not valuable; rather, it means that their value can only be manifested through human perceptions. In the case of American Indians, it means that buffalo took on value because they could provide sustenance, because they could be traded for other goods, or because they had spiritual significance. In each case, however, the values are human values as opposed to buffalo values.

Given that individuals will place different values on resources, the problem for any society is how to discover and balance the competing values and how to generate a system of rewards and penalties for those who achieve that balance. The institutional options are wide-ranging and include private property rights, families, democratic polities, theocratic leadership, and despotic regimes. In the move from the most to the least decentralized institutional forms, the question is: How well does each different institutional arrangement reveal values and channel resources into productive alternatives?

At the most decentralized level of institutions, individuals have control of assets and make decisions about how they will be used. This requires the recognition of individual rights or private property, which are the mainstay of successful economies. The important aspect of individual ownership is that it forces individual decision makers to take account of their actions. If they put an asset to a productive use, they reap the benefits; if they squander the asset, they suffer the consequences. Contrary to popular belief, Indians used varying degrees of private ownership for many assets including household goods, horses, land, and hunting and trapping territories. Prior to the arrival of Europeans, Indians understood the importance of individual rights to property and enforced those rights through formal and informal institutions. This point has been, but should not be, ignored as Indians seek self-determination.

But in all societies, collective decision-making units are also used to decide how values are expressed and to reward and penalize decision makers. For example, families or clans were often central to Indian organization. During battles with other tribes or with whites, the tribe was the central unit for organizing warfare. While hunting in smaller bands, hunting chiefs would coordinate the chase.

Whatever the level of collective activity, collective decisions raise two important problems. First, there is the question of whose values should be represented. In small groups such as the family, this collective aggregation is made easier by the homogeneity of family members. But as the size of the collective expands, aggregation becomes more difficult as a result of heterogeneity and less personal interaction. In modern democracies, voting and politics provide the accepted way of aggregating values, but in primitive societies aggregation often was accomplished through mechanisms such as religious leaders and spiritual visions. A key to the success of these institutions for revelation of values will be how well individuals accept that their own values are being represented. One conclusion is clear from the Indian experience; if a group has a mechanism for aggregating individual values and if a different mechanism is imposed on them without regard for the larger cultural context, the "glue" that binds social contracts may be eroded and the collective decisions rejected.[8] An example of this imposition is provided by the General Allotment Act of 1887, which will be discussed in much more detail later. This act attempted to privatize land on reservations. By allotting land to individual Indians, the federal government imposed a very different institutional structure on Indians who were successfully using the family and tribal structure to organize land use decisions.

> When the Department of the Interior made a conscious policy to break down Indian tribal and family life, these problem-solving structures were broken down as well. This hypothesis accounts for the reduction in Indian wealth that occurred after the allotment period. . . . The irony is that the culture dissolved in its ability to keep order and produce wealth among its members, but this was not accompanied by a transfer of loyalty to white institutions and culture. (Roback, 1992, p. 23)

The experience of tribes on reservations prior to allotment attests to the fact that institutions other than private ownership may be effective in organizing output as long as there is a reward and penalty system supported by the formal and informal institutions.[9]

The second problem with collective decisions is how to

structure the reward and penalty system to encourage productive endeavors. With private decisions, costs and benefits de-
volve to the individual and thus provide appropriate incentives.
Moving the decision-making locus from the individual to the
collective, in the absence of unanimity, increases the likelihood
that the decision-making body can pass along benefits to members of the collective who do not bear the costs. Such coercion
may be necessary to enforce individual rights, or it may provide
a useful way for governments to produce goods that would be
underprovided by individual action. But the same coercive
power also can be used to transfer wealth. The fundamental
problem then becomes how to create collective units that have
the necessary power to protect individual rights and to produce
public goods without that power being used to transfer wealth
to those who control the political power.

> All societies face the problem of preventing those who
> exercise the legitimate powers of government from
> using such power to transfer societal wealth—or ad-
> ditional power—to themselves. . . . Such "rent seek-
> ing" (i.e., the use of power and resources of
> government to enrich those in power rather than to
> add to social wealth) is socially destructive. Not only
> does it unproductively consume resources, but it dis-
> courages investment, particularly in fixed capital
> that cannot flee once it is installed. The task is to limit
> the role of those in power to that of "third party"
> enforcer, rather than self-interested primary party,
> in disputes and social decisions over the use of a
> society's resources. Success at this task stands out as
> a distinguishing characteristic of those sovereign
> nations that have been able to develop economically
> from those that have not. (Cornell & Kalt, 1992a,
> pp. 234–235)

Although the recipe for accomplishing this task is not
complete, it is clear that successful development for Indians
will be related to how well tribal leaders know or can discern
the preferences of tribal members; how accountable the tribal
leaders are to tribal members; and how much competition the
sovereign faces. In cases involving small numbers of people

such as the family, some intimate knowledge of individual values and a desire to do what is "best" for the family unit is presumed. Centralized, hierarchical leadership may also work well when the process for choosing the leader evolves over a long period and selects for leadership traits such as knowledge of the natural environment, preferences of group members, and so on as was the case for pre-European Indian societies. In larger groups with more heterogeneous preferences and more dispersed knowledge among individuals, however, it is difficult for one individual or a small group of individuals to approximate the desires of group members.

The ability of the tribe to hold those who make collective decisions accountable is largely a function of the size of the group and the sociocultural constraints on decision makers. Small societies obviously have an advantage over larger ones on this dimension. In the first place, it is easier in small groups to know what decision makers are doing. Second, with the cost of bad collective decisions shared among a smaller number of people, each member of the group has a stronger incentive to see to it that good collective decisions are made. The typical for-profit firm is the quintessential example of effective monitoring because its performance is measured with profits and its owners bear the costs and reap the benefits of monitoring the firm's agents (see Alchian & Demsetz, 1972). To the extent that Indian tribes are relatively small and live together on reservations, they may closely approximate for-profit firms and should be able to monitor their leaders more effectively.

Accountability is also related to the cultural constraints placed on tribal leaders. For example, contrast the cultural norms of "thou shalt not steal" and "winner take all." The former may constrain agents from using their power to transfer wealth, while the latter may condone any form of wealth transfer. Traditions, rituals, and taboos may constrain the power of charismatic, theocratic leaders. Similarly, for the elected official, the prospect of reelection provides some check on performance. Economists are only beginning to recognize the importance of cultural constraints as an enforcement mechanism in social contracts and have not integrated them into models of economic development. What should become clear from the variety of Indian cultures is that informal cultural constraints may be more effective than formal constitutions or laws at holding tribal leaders accountable.

The third determinant of how successful any society will be at preventing its collective agents from engaging in transfer activity is the ability of individuals to exit from the collective. Like competition in the marketplace, the potential for exit gives citizens an alternative and reduces the coercive power of the collective. After getting the horse, for example, economies of scale in hunting declined, giving individuals a much greater ability to leave the group and strike out on their own. Moreover, where central authority existed, it was usually divided among many different leaders. With war chiefs in charge of fighting and hunt chiefs in charge of obtaining food, there was less potential for any single leader to gain much power to transfer wealth. Once relegated to reservations, however, tribal governments combined with Bureau of Indian Affairs (BIA) authority added strength and power to centralized government and limited the alternatives for individuals. To exit from tribal and BIA power, the individual Indian must leave the reservation and integrate into non-Indian society. In the absence of exit alternatives, those who control the legitimate powers of government will be much more capable of using those powers to transfer wealth to themselves.

Given that the fundamental problem facing all societies is how to constrain the collective to its legitimate productive activities, calling for self-determination is not enough to ensure successful progress for Indians. If tribes can find the right balance between formal and informal institutions for channeling collective powers into productive endeavors, development is more likely. Where informal, cultural constraints remain strong, they can complement other collective constraints to encourage productive activity. Unfortunately, years of federal control have eroded some of the informal institutions that traditionally constrained collective leaders, making the problem of self-determination all the more difficult. Some tribal councils have been notorious for their corruption despite formal constitutions and laws. Indeed, it is precisely this institutional setting that must be changed if self-determination is to improve economic performance on reservations. The difficult task on Indian lands is changing this institutional setting.

Institutional Change

Knowing how and why institutions change helps us understand how Indians got where they are and how they might change institutions in the future. The rules of the game are produced through human action that depends on the benefits and costs of producing or changing the rules. To take an important resource in the arid West, consider the rules that determine who has the right to derive wealth from water that flows across Indian reservations. Late in the nineteenth century when white farmers and miners were settling the American West, they understood that for water to be valuable, it would have to be moved from the stream to the farm lands or mining areas. Because water law in the East did not allow diversion from the stream, the rules had to change to accommodate the needs of settlers. As a result, the prior appropriation doctrine evolved establishing water rights on the basis of first-in-time, first-in-right. This institution says that the person who first appropriates water by diverting it has the first right to the amount appropriated. Therefore, in dry years, the most senior water demands must be met first, the next most senior demands next, and so on. Since water generally was put to use first by white farmers and miners, they established senior rights to this precious resource.[10]

When Indians tried to use water early in the twentieth century, conflicts arose that were eventually resolved through the Winters doctrine (*Winters v. United States,* 207 U.S. 564 [1980]). Indians on the Fort Belknap Reservation tried to use water that had been claimed by white irrigators. The non-Indian irrigators went to court arguing that they had a senior water right that precluded Indian use. The court reasoned that "it would be extreme to believe that . . . Congress . . . took from [the Indians] the means of continuing their old habits, yet did not leave them the power to change to new ones." Hence, it ruled that establishment of reservations also established water rights sufficient to irrigate the arable acreage of the reservation. Of course, what constitutes the "practicable irrigable acreage," the standard used to quantify Indian rights, has generated tremendous debate in subsequent court cases.

But the efforts by Indians in the Winters case did change the rules of the game governing water, although the Winters doctrine went unenforced for many years.[11]

What drove the efforts to change water institutions for Indians and whites alike was the increasing value of the resource. Similarly, as land, minerals, timber, oil, and other resources have risen in value, parties have attempted to establish rights to them. Hence, the history of the American West— for Indians and whites alike—is a history of these efforts. Wilkinson notes that "the tribes have repeatedly raised arguments that implicitly rest upon a tribal right to change, to evolve from the kinds of legal institutions and societies that existed in aboriginal times or when the treaties and treaty substitutes were negotiated" (1987, p. 68).

Even before interaction with Europeans, Indian institutions were evolving as a result of changing resource values and technology. Perhaps as much as any other factor, the horse changed the lives of Indians. With the horse, transportation costs declined significantly as did the costs of harvesting buffalo. The result was that many otherwise sedentary tribes took to a more nomadic life, pursuing buffalo over wide territories. As the horse technology combined with the growing European market for hides and furs, issues of who owned horses and who had hunting rights became paramount. Subsequent chapters will illustrate that Indians had a rich history of institutional evolution, suggesting that they were very capable of responding to the benefits and costs of changing the rules of the game. This ability to evolve and adapt has been ignored in modern efforts to lock Indians into a cultural time warp that assumes aboriginal societies had static institutions.

One important variable in the institutional change equation over which the Indians had little control was the U.S. Congress. To the extent that Congress was making the rules on behalf of white constituents, the benefits and costs to Indians of alternative institutions were often of little relevance. For example, the Dawes Act of 1887 (otherwise known as the General Allotment Act), which assigned parcels of land to individual Indians, may have been designed to give Indians the benefits of private ownership. But an explanation more consistent with modern theories of political economy is that it provided a mechanism for land hungry whites to obtain access to reservations and for bureaucrats to expand their domains. In this framework, benefits and costs are calculated very differently from those in a private context, because government has the power to dictate who bears the costs and who reap the benefits. Not surprisingly, there is no guarantee that the institutions that evolve will generate efficiency or equity. For this reason, Cornell and Kalt believe that

> the prospects for survival of the federal Indian bureaucracy are inversely related to the successful development and empowerment of American Indian tribes. The bureaucracy's funding agency, the U.S. Congress, responds to a broader non-Indian constituency's willingness to allocate resources to perceived Indian problems. This demand appears to rise as those problems become more severe. This places the Indian bureaucracy, interested in the size of its budgets and span of its control, in the position of marketing poverty to Congress. It has done this well. (1992a, p. 217)

In this setting, it should not be surprising that Indian economies have not performed well.

Economic Performance

By understanding institutions and institutional change we can improve our chances of understanding why poverty has persisted on American Indian reservations. For many years, economists have searched for the recipe that would bring progress to less developed economies, and the history of American Indian policy reflects this search. Based on the notion that the industrial revolution was stimulated by capital investment, the first ingredient in the recipe for success became capital. The federal government has tried to provide capital to reservation economies under the assumption that economic growth would follow. Between 1936 and 1970, BIA loans and loan guarantees for economic development totaled $94.6 million. By 1984, an additional $171.3 million in direct loans had been made, and a total of $137.9 million in private loans had been guaranteed (U.S.

Department of the Interior, 1986, p. 83). Though it is arguable that these sums simply have not been large enough and that some direct and indirect economic gains have arisen from these programs, it is generally recognized that the rate of return on these investments has been dismally low.

The second ingredient thrown into the development kettle was human capital. As with physical capital, there is good evidence that successful economies have made important investments in human capital. Hence, the reservation war on poverty was fought with expenditures on education and health care. Even at the outset of the reservation experiment, Indian agents of the BIA were engaged in teaching the basics of modern agriculture. The early attention to education is reflected in Article 6 of the Navajo treaty of 1868:

> In order to insure the civilization of the Indians entering into this treaty, the necessity of education is admitted, especially of such of them as may be settled on said agricultural parts of this reservation, and they therefore pledge themselves to compel their children, male and female, between the ages of six and sixteen years, to attend school; and it is hereby made the duty of the agent for said Indians to see that this stipulation is strictly complied with; and the United States agrees that, for every thirty children between said ages who can be induced or compelled to attend school, a house shall be provided, and a teacher competent to teach the elementary branches of an English education shall be furnished, who will reside. (quoted in Kappler, 1904, 2, p. 1017)

In the 1960s, the BIA lost some of its influence over Indian education policy as other agencies such as the Office of Economic Opportunity, the Indian Health Service (Department of Health, Education and Welfare), the Economic Development Administration, and the Comprehensive Employment and Training Administration (CETA) began providing on-the-job training, work experience, technical assistance, health care, and youth employment. The 1986 *Report of the Task Force on Indian Economic Development* summed up this trend:

Beginning with the war-on-poverty, the Federal government made a major commitment to improve the economic circumstances of Indian reservations. Initially, much of the effort was devoted to providing investment capital, manpower training, technical assistance and other assistance designed to promote more vigorous—and hopefully at some point self-sustaining—economies on Indian reservations. (U.S. Department of the Interior, 1986, p. 90)

As shown in Table 1.1, the result of this war on poverty was that approximately $3 billion was being spent on Indian programs by the mid-1980s. Given an Indian population of slightly more than 300,000, this amounts to about $9000 per capita.

Despite these federal expenditures on physical and human capital, studies generally indicated that "the programs were providing large amounts of money which were generating sub-

TABLE 1.1 Total Federal Funding for Indian Programs, by Department for Selected Fiscal Years (millions of dollars)

	1973	1981	1982	1983	1984	1985
Agriculture	$26.6	$49.0	$89.4	$85.4	$85.3	$74.8
Commerce	31.1	24.0	14.5	4.7	7.8	10.4
Education	–	334.0	240.2	299.8	328.1	325.0
Energy	–	–	.8	.8	.5	.5
HHS	404.3	729.0	744.3	838.6	916.7	957.7
HUD	34.8	321.0	598.5	402.7	484.3	320.2*
Interior	503.4	1,120.0	1,022.6	1,173.6	1,025.8	1,079.4
Labor	47.9	157.0	90.1	91.9	135.3	75.4
Transportation**	–	–	1.2	76.4	100.5	100.5
Treasury	–	11.0	11.2	11.2	11.2	11.2
EPA	–	–	5.1	5.3	.3	.5
SBA	19.8	–	2.8	9.0	7.7	2.6
Totals	1,067.9	2,745.0	2,820.7	2,999.4	3,103.5	2,958.1

Notes: * Estimate only. ** Responsibility for road construction on reservations transferred from BIA to the Department of Transportation in 1983. However, BIA continues to set priorities in the allocation of these funds.

Source: U.S. Department of the Interior (1986, p. 88).

stantial jobs and income for Indians on reservations, and having other benefits, but that the programs were not having much success in creating viable and self-sustaining economies on these reservations" (U.S. Department of the Interior, 1986, p. 78).

So the search for the magic growth recipe continues, with the focus turning increasingly to institutions. The simple fact is that *incentives matter*—whether considering the former Soviet Union, IBM, or the Crow tribe. To understand why economies grow or stagnate, the first step is to understand what incentives the institutions produce. If individuals or groups are rewarded for investments in physical or human capital, these investments are more likely to grow. On the other hand, if there is a higher return to lobbying government to obtain wealth transfers, potentially productive efforts will be diverted to this alternative. As noted earlier, such activities are not only counterproductive in their incentive effects but consume resources that could be used more productively. These activities also involve confrontational politics and tear at the social fabric.

In this regard, recent Indian policy has been counterproductive. "The Federal commitment to assist Indians has turned ... towards the direct provision of goods and services," with the unintended adverse consequence that "Indians have been left perhaps even more dependent than before on the Federal government for income, employment and general provision for their economic welfare. Indians are subject to swings in the political fortunes of the Federal programs on which they now depend" (U.S. Department of the Interior, 1986, p. 90). If Indians wish to influence the "swings in political fortunes," they must play the transfer game.

As already noted, the failure of Indian policy to provide self-sustaining, self-determined economies has been blamed on differences between cultures. In discussing early policies, Taylor notes that "Indian agents and missionary groups made sincere efforts to train Indians in mechanical and agricultural pursuits," concluding that "the lack of results from these efforts was largely due to cultural differences" (1984, p. 16). Regarding more recent policy, labor economists Levitan and Johnston state that "although continuing heavy funding may quiet the critics by raising standards of living on reservations, money will not resolve the more difficult remaining problems. These thorny issues have to do with fundamental cultural differences and with the basic status of Indians on reservations" (1975, pp. 73–74).

Certainly culture cannot be left out of the institutional milieu, because culture is itself a crucial part of the informal institutions. But it will not suffice to conclude that the lack of growth is due to Indians being different. Culture is but one of many variables that make up institutions. It may condition social interaction in ways that are difficult for people from other cultures to understand (for example, religious ceremonies), but culture never completely overrides the individual ego. Culture may induce the individual to set aside self-interest at some cost to him or herself, but as that cost rises, we can expect this tendency to decline. At some point, individual incentives will matter. Moreover, like it or not, our society is set within a melting pot of cultures known as America, and this culture has had an impact on Indians. All around reservations are people with better housing, transportation, diets, health, longevity, clothing, and the list goes on. Indian culture may induce individual Indians to accept fewer material goods in return for spiritual well-being, while western culture brings opposite pressures. Regardless of whether this is good or bad, the question is: How can Indians best manage their own lives to attain the balance they desire? This is what self-determination is all about.

But self-determination has not characterized Indian policy for more than a century. Beginning with the General Allotment Act in 1887, Congress attempted to legislate the institutions under which Indian resources would be managed. Initially, allotment was aimed at private ownership, with the idea that Indians would be more productive on their own lands. Today few doubt the efficacy of private property in stimulating productivity and, in fact, I will provide data in Chapter 6 showing that agricultural productivity on privately owned reservation lands is much higher than on Indian land with other tenures. Regardless of Indian culture before the arrival of Europeans, this fact cannot be ignored. By the same token, private property ownership is not the only institution that could improve productivity on reservations. Prior to allotment, Carlson (1992) has shown that Indians were relying on communal institutions to increase agricultural productivity. But the communal institutions that were used early in the reservation period or prior to confinement to reservations were not a romantic form of Marx's "from each according to his ability, to each according to his needs." These communal institutions included incentives and constraints for individuals. In the chapters that follow, the focus will be on the rules of the game, the incentives they generate, and the ways in which they change.

Notes

1. Dorner (1961) and Sorkin (1971) come to similar conclusions for earlier periods.

2. For further discussion of the "murky concept" of multiculturalism, see Royal (1992).

3. For a recent argument regarding the alien nature of markets to American Indian societies, see Champagne (1992).

4. For details on the general applicability of this approach see North (1990) and Eggertsson (1990). For a specific application to Indian problems, see Anderson (1992) and Cornell and Kalt (1992a).

5. This three-part approach follows the title and format of North (1990).

6. This conclusion is counter to that of Cornell and Kalt (1992a, p. 244) who "are not sanguine about the possibility of invisible-hand theories of the development of informal, cultural institutions."

7. See Lueck (1993) for a discussion of similar results in other cases where formal institutions from central governments have replaced informal institutions.

8. See Cornell and Kalt (1992a, p. 218) for more discussion of this cultural "glue."

9. For further discussion, see Chapter 6. Also, see Roback (1992, p. 9) for a more complete discussion of the optimal locus of authority given different cultural constraints. She argues "that resources should be privatized over the group size that can best internalize the relevant externalities." It then becomes an empirical question as to whether the optimal size is the individual, the family, or centralized government.

10. For a complete discussion of the evolution of property rights to water, see Anderson and Hill (1975).

11. For a discussion of the benefits and costs of using the Winters doctrine relative to the benefits and costs of negotiating settlements over water disputes, see Smith (1992).

C H A P T E R   2

The Red Man's Law

It is difficult to fit pre-Columbian Indian institutions into the modern context of law, government, and property rights. For example, the term *nation* is applied to Indian tribes as if the tribes were organized into formal governing structures for the entire group of Indians similar to governments that manage modern nation states. But generally Indian tribes were made up of relatively independent groups with little centralized control except at specific times when the bands might gather for such events as ceremonies or hunts. Describing the Yurok Indians who lived on the Klamath River in the Pacific Northwest, Goldsmidt finds that "we may dismiss the village and tribe with a word. Though persons were identified by their village of residence and their tribe of origin, neither of these groups had any direct claim upon the action of the individual. There was no village nor national government, no village or tribal action in wars" (1951, p. 511). Similarly, formal laws as codified by modern legislatures had little relevance in premodern societies that seldom had a written language to communicate such laws. In addition, the modern notion of private property rights as well-defined ownership enforced by governmental institutions and traded in the marketplace had little application in aboriginal societies where individual rights were defended by closely knit social groups and where formal markets were lacking.

Nonetheless, the lack of formal institutions by no means implies that Indians lacked rules, customary or formal, that are a necessary component of orderly life. As Hoebel put it, "primitive anarchy does not mean disorder" (1954, p. 294). If the "major role of institutions in a society is to reduce uncertainty by establishing a stable . . . structure to human interaction" (North, 1990, p. 6), American Indian societies were quite successful. Customs evolved over long periods, allowing Indians to survive and prosper. Archaeological evidence of tribes along the Pacific Northwest coast and civilizations in the Southwest suggests that these Indians were able to produce and sustain abundant wealth and technology. As you shall see in this chapter, life among the various groups of North American Indians was anything but chaotic and disorderly, but it was seldom ruled by strong centralized forms of governance.

Posner sums up the tendency for evolution toward institutions that promote productive activities and wealth creation in tribal societies.

> It is actually easier to explain why efficiency would have great social survival value in the primitive world than to explain this for our world. The efficient society is wealthier than the inefficient—that is what efficiency means—and a wealthier society will support a larger population. This effect of greater wealth can be decisive in the competition among primitive societies, where the methods of warfare are simple and numbers of people count for much more than in modern warfare. Archaic societies sufficiently durable to have left substantial literary or archaeological remains and primitive societies sufficiently durable to have survived into the nineteenth century . . . are likely, therefore, to be societies whose customs are efficient. (1980, p. 53)

In this chapter, I will consider the extent to which the institutions of pre-Columbian Indians were efficient. Did the rules of the game force decision-making units, be they individual or collective, to take account of the costs and benefits of their actions? Did the rules encourage efforts to increase wealth or to redistribute it? Because "institutions affect the performance of the economy by their effect on costs of exchange and production" (North, 1990, p. 5), institutions can be judged on the extent to which they reduce these costs. Hence, if individuals or groups are rewarded for cooperating with others, for generating good information about resource constraints, for conserving scarce resources, and for innovating and implementing new technologies, it is more likely that the society will prosper.

None of this implies that individual self-interest will not be conditioned by other factors, such as customs, culture, and ideologies. To the extent that social groups, especially families, can inculcate in their members a willingness to sacrifice self-interest for group interest,[1] the costs of organizing collective action, such as hunting or warfare, will be reduced. Collective action always confronts the free-rider problem, wherein individuals can withhold effort from the collective action and still enjoy the fruits of its production. Therefore, for collective action to be effective, the free-rider problem must be overcome. Developing ideologies that induce individuals to resist taking a free ride despite obvious personal gains can conserve on valuable resources necessary for group production and cohesion. Otherwise, resources must be expended to force people to contribute, and this can tear at the social fabric.

Inculcating a willingness to sacrifice individual self-interest for group interest can also be important for reducing the costs of enforcing property rights. In western societies, the commandment that "thou shalt not steal" is taught in churches and by families and has the effect of reducing theft. Clearly such a commandment is not sufficient to prevent all theft, and resources must be devoted to policing. But in the absence of any adherence to this norm, policing costs would be much higher. Such norms are more likely to be effective in small, closely knit, homogeneous societies, which explains why norms played an important role amongst American Indians.

Though there is no general theory of how such ideologies evolve or under what circumstances they work, it is clear that population growth beyond families and clans and interaction with other cultures weakens the ties derived from personal interaction.[2] Under these circumstances, institutions that rely on collective coercion must be used to force individuals to fully account for their actions. Even in families, one of the smallest social groups, self-interest will prevail at times and require collective coercion. It is argued that "because of their cultural heritage, American Indians have a special relationship to all things, a oneness or unity of body and spirit that has made it possible for them to endure unbelievable hardships and oppression" (Timmons, 1980, p. ix). While cultural heritage is an important behavioral factor in any society, a full understanding of the American Indian's "relationship to all things" must include the role of formal and informal institutions in constraining individual behavior. The remainder of this chapter will be devoted to examples of American Indian institutions that served to internalize costs and benefits of individual action; that is, to get the incentives right.

Order without Law[3]

Institutions ranging from individual private property rights to organized formal governments are used by all societies to condition individual behavior. At the most decentralized level, the individual sanctions him or herself through a set of personal ethics and exercises self-control to abide by those ethics. In this context, there may be "a oneness or unity of body and spirit that has made it possible for them [Indians] to endure unbelievable hardships and oppression" (Timmons, 1980, p. ix). For example, "private citizens may become vigilantes who use self-help to enforce substantive legal rules. Conversely, police officers may often apply norms and personal ethics, not 'the book,' in their everyday work" (Ellickson, 1991, p. 132). But this is only part of the matrix of social control.

As individuals interact in groups, they engage in contracts with one another. Contracts that allow the parties to avail themselves of gains from trade also present the prospect that one party may shirk on promised action, capturing gains at the expense of the other. At this stage of interaction, individual sanctions will be insufficient, and collective sanctions become necessary. These sanctions could come from individuals banding together with friends or family to enforce contracts against others as was common among aboriginal societies. This form of self-help "literally denotes an individual's efforts to administer sanctions in his own behalf" (Ellickson, 1991, p. 131, fn.21). In the traditional legal and sociological context, it includes "sanctions administered by friends, relatives, gossips, vigilantes, and other nonhierarchical third-party enforcers" (p. 131, fn. 21). Such self-help was an important part of the Indians' institutional mix.

Sanctions for everyday activities that occurred in smaller social groups often relied on self-help. Speaking of the Basin-Plateau Indian groups, Steward observes that "political groups and chiefs had no interest in disputes, criminal or civil, between individuals. These were settled by relatives, usually close kin" (1938, p. 246). Because the Plains tribes lacked any centralized authority, law, or judiciary except during communal activities, "every person is thus constituted his own judge, jury and executioner" (Denig, 1930, p. 480). According to Lowie, "most difficulties were settled by individuals and their kindred" (1920, p. 415) for offenses such as adultery, homicide, trespass, assault, and theft. Hoebel summarizes the decentralized nature of social sanctions this way: "The community group, although it may be ethnologically a segment of a tribe, is autonomous and politically independent. There is no tribal state. Leadership resides in family or local group headmen who have little coercive authority and are hence lacking in both the means to exploit and the means to judge" (1954, p. 294).

Benson (1992) documents further evidence that sanctions among American Indians generally relied on less centralized mechanisms. Among the Yurok Indians of the Pacific Northwest, offenses including murder, adultery, theft, poaching, curses, and even minor insults could be prosecuted by following specific legal procedures. The offended party

> would hire two, three, or four "crossers"—nonrelatives from a community other than his own. The defendant in the claim would also hire crossers, and the entire group hired by both parties would act as go-betweens, ascertaining claims and defenses and gathering evidence. The crossers would render a

judgement for damages after hearing all the evidence. (Benson, 1992, p. 29)

If the crossers found the defendant guilty, restitution had to be paid. "Every invasion of person or property was valued in terms of property, and each required exact compensation. Again, law was clearly in the nature of modern tort law rather than criminal law" (p. 30), except that sanctions were enforced through self-help rather than through the coercive powers of a central government.

The Comanche had no centralized political unit to sanction social control. According to Hoebel, "the tribe was no more than a congeries of bands held together as a peace group by the bonds of common tongue and culture. There appears to have been no machinery for institutionalized political action on a tribal scale" (1954, p. 184). They depended on "peace chiefs" who were band headmen but who had no "law-speaking or law-enforcing authority" (p. 133).

Instead, the peace chiefs provided a clearing house for information passed from generation to generation. Steward (1938) describes the chief in the Basin-Plateau Indian context as one who

> was principally to keep informed about the ripening of plant foods in different localities, to impart his information to the villagers, and if all the families traveled to the same pine-nut area, to manage the trip and help arrange where each was to harvest. As a "talker," he gave long orations, telling of his information and giving directions to families who cared to cooperate. His authority, however, was not absolute. Any family was at liberty to pursue an independent course at any time. (p. 247)

"Anyone who did not like his [the chief's] decision simply ignored it. If in time a good many people ignored his announcements and preferred to stay behind with some other man of influence, or perhaps to move in another direction with other men, the chief has lost his following" (Hoebel, 1954, p. 132). In this spontaneous competition, those who provided the best information retained their position of power and influence.

Larger group interaction should increase the use of more formal, centralized structures to impose sanctions against those who harm others or those who attempt to free ride. The increase in formal structures should be positively related to

- the heterogeneity of the group,
- the size of the group, and
- the likelihood that individual and group interests might diverge with an activity as in the case of war.

In Provinse's description of Plains Indian culture, the underlying sanctions follow this pattern, with specific sanctions depending on "(1) the nature of the attitudes and beliefs aroused by the act calling the sanction into operation and (2) the existence and nature of the machinery by which society responds to the delinquent's acts" (1955, pp. 343–344). Where groups were homogeneous, diffuse sanctions depended on ridicule, praise, humor, honor, and disgrace as means of expressing approval or disapproval for violating or abiding by social norms (pp. 355–365). In addition, religious taboos provided incentives for scouts in the buffalo hunt to tell the truth regarding the location of buffalo or face "dire consequences, such as being struck by lightning, thrown by one's horse, bitten by a snake" (p. 360).

When communal activities generated the potential for free-rider problems or shirking by individuals, third-party sanctions imposed through a centralized authority were more common. For example, in group hunting activities it was imperative that individuals act in unison. Ewers captures the difference between sanctions in large and small groups: "If the camp was a tribal one, the chief . . . proclaimed that the prohibition against individual hunting was in force. I gained the impression that this regulation was less common in the smaller band camps" (1969, p. 155).

Ordinarily, "a chief's authority was restricted to certain definite activities, such as hunts, dances, war, or ceremonies" (Steward 1938, p. 246). Indian police or soldiers themselves were sanctioned by social norms and personal ethics. The police were used in conjunction with specific occasions "(1) to regulate the communal hunt; (2) to regulate tribal ceremonies; (3) to settle disputes, punish offenders, and preserve order in camp;

and (4) to regulate war parties and restrain such at inopportune times" (Provinse, 1955, p. 351). On such occasions, coordination proved essential, and free riding or shirking could not be tolerated. When engaging in war, the Omaha police "acted to keep order while the party was in movement, guarding against surprise attacks, restraining the overzealous, urging on the stragglers, and insuring that no one left the group without proper authority" (p. 347), and when hunting "the policemen were empowered to strike those who 'quarreled and fought, stole, or scared off the buffalo'" (p. 349). Without such authority, Indians would have had to rely solely on personal ethics, social norms, or self-enforcement. That they could not and did not suggests that their "oneness or unity of body and spirit" was not sufficient for survival.

In summary, American Indian societies were not without institutions to ensure order. Sanctions often depended on self-help to ensure that order prevailed. More centralized authority was used when groups were less homogeneous, when groups were larger, and when communal activities could not tolerate free riders. Benson (1992) summarizes the characteristics of Indian legal systems prior to the arrival and continual westward movement of Europeans:

> They are: (1) rules of conduct that emphasized a predominant concern for individual rights and private property, (2) the responsibility of law enforcement falling to the victim backed by reciprocal arrangements for protection and support when a dispute arose, (3) standard adjudicative procedures established to avoid violent forms of dispute resolution, (4) offenses treated as torts punishable by economic payments in restitution, and (5) strong incentives to yield to prescribed punishment when guilty of an offense due to the reciprocally established threat of social ostracism which led to physical retribution. (p. 32)

Indian law was based not so much on powerful individuals or groups who had the coercive power to impose the law but rather on the reciprocal expectations of individuals who depended on one another.

The Common Law of Indian Property

"How can you buy or sell the sky, the warmth of the land?" Chief Seattle reportedly asked in a now famous speech delivered in the 1850s.[4] This is the beginning of the legend that private ownership was inimical to an Indian culture that revered nature and her bounty. The words in the oft-quoted speech, however, are not actually those of Chief Seattle. Rather, they are the words of Ted Perry, who paraphrased classical scholar William Arrowsmith's translation of the speech. Perry's version added "a good deal more, particularly modern ecological imagery" (Wilson, 1992, p. 1457). Though it was Perry and not Chief Seattle who wrote that "every part of the Earth is sacred to my people," the underlying philosophy has been taken as historical evidence that personal ethics sanctioned by self-control prevented Indians from despoiling nature and fouling their environment.

This legend or myth notwithstanding, Huffman (1992) concludes that:

> it is not entirely true that Native Americans knew nothing of ownership. The language of the common law of property, like all of the English language, was unfamiliar to them. But the concepts of the tenancy in common was not foreign to bands and tribes who claimed and defended entitlements to hunting and fishing grounds. Nor was the concept of fee simple title alien to Native American individuals who possessed implements of war and peace, and even lands from which others could be excluded. (p. 907)

Though care must be taken not to overextend modern notions of property to aboriginal societies, it does not follow from the lack of these concepts that only Chief Seattle's philosophy conditioned resource use. To the extent that resources were scarce, survival did depend on rules or customs that determined who had access to and use of these resources.

If personal ethics was an important part of Indian society, it worked along with private and communal property rights that limited access to scarce resources. Examples of pre-

Columbian Indian property rights suggestive of the richness of Indian social control mechanisms can be found in relation to land, hunting and fishing territories, and personal property.

Land

In his seminal article on the evolution of property rights, Demsetz noted that among most Indian tribes "there did not exist anything resembling private ownership in land" (1967, p. 352). Referring to the migratory tribes of the Basin-Plateau, Steward (1938) confirms Demsetz's conclusion:

> All natural resources, with the sole exception of privately owned eagle nests, were free to any one. This was not communal ownership; it was not ownership at all, because no groups whatever claimed natural resources. Water, seed, and hunting areas, mineral and salt deposits, etc., were freely utilized by anyone.[5] (p. 253)

Certainly among the nomadic Plains tribes that roamed in pursuit of buffalo, ownership of land made little sense, though each tribe did have roughly defined geographic regions within which it hunted.

The rich anthropological literature on America's Indians provides fertile soil for discovering why and how property rights varied among Indians. In the Southeast, where Indians were more accustomed to settled agriculture, private ownership of land was common.

> The Creek town is typical of the economic and social life of the populous tribes of the Southeast. . . . Each family gathered the produce of its own plot and placed it in its own storehouse. Each also contributed voluntarily to a public store which was kept in a large building in the field and was used under the direction of the town chief for public needs. The Cherokee town had similar economic, social, and political organization. (Debo, 1970, pp. 13–14)

Private garden plots were common in the East as were large community fields with plots assigned to individual families. Because there were economies of scale in planting and cultivation, these tasks were done communally under the direction of a chief, but harvesting on each plot was done by the owning family with the bounty stored in the family's own storehouse.

In contrast, the Great Basin Shoshone, a group often portrayed as one of the poorest and most primitive, did not have an elaborately developed cultural system or social organization. Dry soil and low rainfall dictated that agriculture was impossible without irrigation. Instead, the Shoshone subsisted on a diet of roots, berries, nuts, plants, fish, antelope, and grasshoppers, depending on what nature provided during a particular season. Because of their constant search for alternative food supplies in an environment with high variability and low average food productivity, the Shoshone were a nomadic tribe that lived together in extended nuclear families with the total population dispersed over a wide area.[6] According to Debo, the Indians of the Great Basin and the California desert areas were a sociable people who gathered occasionally for communal ceremonies, dances, and hunts, "but they had no organized tribal governments" (1970, p. 17).

Indian land tenure systems varied from tribe to tribe and location to location, "ranging from completely or almost completely communal systems to systems hardly less individualistic than our own with its core of fee simple tenure" (Copper, 1949, p. 1). Tribes that practiced sedentary agriculture definitely recognized exclusive land use. The Machican Indians in the Northeast possessed hereditary usufruct rights to well-defined tracts of garden land along the rivers. "This was understood as ownership by the Europeans, who usually approached lineage leaders for land purchase" (Brasser, 1974, p. 14), as recorded in deeds of white settlers in the region. Even other Indians recognized Machican ownership. Farther from the rivers, however, "lineage tracts were vague; no one would consider laying out a garden in the rocky hinterlands" (p. 7).

The Hopi and Zuni branches of the Pueblo Indians living in the Upper Colorado Basin also developed property rights consistent with their environment and production techniques. The Hopi faced an arid climate but were able to make use of periodic flooding of their lands during the summer months. By building small stone walls to check the flow of water, the Hopi prevented flooding of their crops and enhanced soil moisture.

Scale economies in the construction of the irrigation systems made communal production and ownership of the dams superior to individual effort and ownership. These flood waters, controlled and delivered in communal irrigation systems, were shared. But in cases where water flowed constantly from springs on individually owned land and required little or no investment, water rights were privately owned.

The flood control and irrigation systems developed by the Pueblo Indians required extensive capital investments and an elaborate institutional structure, including communal and private property. "Technically the irrigated farmlands belonged to the Pueblo as a whole. Through assignment by the Isleta governor, an individual usually obtained a single acre of land [and the necessary water rights], but if the governor or his captains found that the assignee left the land within a year or did not farm it, the plot and accompanying water rights were returned to Pueblo possession and reassigned" (Ellis, 1979, p. 355). The Havasupai also considered private ownership of farmland as long as it was in use, and the Hopi Indians assigned exclusive rights to the fields to various matrilineal clans of the village. "Each clan allotment was marked by boundary stones, set up at the corners of the fields, with symbols of the clans painted on them" (Kennard, 1979, p. 554). Forde also notes that clan lands were marked "by numerous boundary stones . . . placed at the corners and junctions points" and "engraved on their faces with symbols of the appropriate clan" (1931, p. 367). The clan allotments were usually assigned to the women and became associated with a specific household through inheritance. To spread the risk associated with lack of rain or sudden flooding, each clan generally had plots in more than one location.[7] "Dispersal of the lands of each clan over a number of sites is of very great practical importance since it reduces the risk of crop failure; where one group of fields may be washed out there remains the chance that the others may be spared" (Forde, 1931, p. 369). The success of the Hopi institutional structure is summarized by Forde:

> Hopi agriculture thus presents a number of remarkable characters which serve to mitigate the severity of an arid environment. By careful adaptation to local

conditions and by the use of ingenious but unelaborate devices all the characteristic plants of the American maize-squash complex are successfully cultivated on a considerable scale. Agriculture is not, as often in marginal regions, auxiliary to hunting and collecting, but basic in the economy. (p. 399)

Fruit and nut trees that required long-term investment and care were privately owned and usually inherited.[8] "So important were the piñon resources that groves of trees were considered family property in several locations" within the Great Basin (Fowler, 1986, p. 65). In one case, a Northern Paiute reflected that his father "paid a horse for a certain piñon-nut range" (Stewart 1941, p. 440), suggesting that the property rights were valuable and could be traded. Grazing rights, on the other hand, were usually held in common due to the cost of containing livestock and the variance in fodder over the range.

California Indians also recognized property rights to land. "Land, among Owens Valley Paiute and, to a lesser extent, among Salinas Valley Shoshone, was band-owned and defended against trespass" (Steward, 1941, p. 254). California Shoshone populations were comparatively more dense than the Great Basin Shoshone and were much more sedentary. Their land was fertile, providing conditions necessary for agriculture, enabling a more sedentary lifestyle usually organized in permanent villages. The result was a system of enforceable private property rights supported by a degree of organized tribal control. "Ecology thus permitted, if it did not cause, band development" (Steward, 1938, p. 258). Named, landowning bands lived under the direction of chiefs with well-defined authority. Band unity was reinforced by communal sweat houses and mourning ceremonies. Families owned piñon, mesquite, screw-bean trees, and a few wild-seed patches, with ownership "being marked off by lines of rocks" (Lowie, 1940, p. 303). Though permission to gather food was sometimes given during times of abundance, trespass was not tolerated, "the owner rebuking him [the trespasser] with such words as, 'Don't pick pine nuts here! They are not yours, but mine'" (p. 303). At the extreme, John Muir reports that the owner of a piñon tree killed a white man for felling his tree (reported in Steward, 1934, p. 305).[9]

Of course, the degree of private ownership varied according to scarcity and according to the difficulty of defining and enforcing rights. Because agricultural land required investments and because boundaries could be marked easily, it was more common for the lands to be privately owned. Where enforcement did take place, it was not carried out by centralized authorities but generally relied on self-help with the family, clan, or village. Nomadic tribes found little use for institutions of land ownership, but this does not mean that they did not recognize property rights. Steward concludes that "truly communal property was scant" (1938, p. 253) among American Indians.

Tenancy in common as well as fee simple ownership were found among most agricultural tribes. Especially in cases where capital investment was required for irrigation, cultivation, or husbanding, Indians defined and enforced individual or family property rights to land.

Fishing and Hunting Territories

Since Indians depended so much on hunting and fishing, it was imperative that they carefully manage those resources. As long as game was plentiful, there was little need for concern, but if abundance declined because of natural conditions or competition from other users, the potential for overuse was of paramount concern. Though private ownership of the fish or animals themselves was impossible because of the migratory nature of wildlife (see Lueck, 1993), Indians recognized the importance of controlling access to general hunting territories and to specific harvest sights.

The complexity of Indian territorial hunting rights in the far North is discussed by Usher. He notes that while the "Inuit have often expressed generous sentiments with respect to their land, such as 'the land belongs to everyone,' 'the land is large and there is room for everyone,' or 'it is everybody's country,'" the fact is that the Inuit "had definite concepts about the territorial rights and limits of the tribe and band, as well as systems of tenure and allocation within these groups" (1992, p. 46). Much like land rights farther to the south, territorial hunting rights in the North arose through use and occupancy, and outsiders were often allowed to use the area for a short period of time. Customs and norms promoted conservation by regulating the manner in which individuals hunted, trapped, and fished.

> That these systems of customary law were rarely committed to writing . . . is not proof that they did not exist. No individual did exactly as he pleased in some lawless jungle where the strong triumphed over the weak. . . . These rules were often expressed in terms of religion and spirituality rather than of science as we understand it today. Nonetheless, the rules conserved the resource base and harmony within the band. (Usher, 1992, p. 50)

Hunting groups among the Montagnais-Naskapi of Quebec between Hudson Bay and the Gulf of Saint Lawrence recognized particular "'hunting areas,' and as furbearers, especially beaver, became important trade items, regularized access to such areas took on new significance" (Rogers & Taylor, 1981, p. 181). Where disputes over territories occurred, there is no evidence that they relied on any organized political units for settlement but rather settled them through self-help. This often involved a hunting group that formed the primary social unit.

Similar hunting groups and rules existed in other regions. Quoting Indian informants, Speck and Hadlock report that for New Brunswick, "It was . . . an established 'rule that when a hunter worked a territory no other would knowingly or willfully encroach upon the region for several generations.' Some of the men held districts which had been hunted by their fathers, and presumably their grandfathers" (1946, p. 362). They even had a colloquial term that translates to "my hunting ground," this "being a literal rendering of its verbal stem" (p. 362). As Juergensmayer and Wadley note, "had they cared . . . [the colonists] would have found considerable land area already vested with ownership concepts understandable to them as 'common land,' and other lands clothed with 'rights of common,' particularly fishing and hunting rights" (1974, p. 372). Speck (1939) believes that the Algonkian Indians from the Atlantic to the Great Lakes were "aboriginal conservators" because they carried on their hunting in restricted, family hunting territories descending from generation to generation in the male line. It was in these family tracts that the supply of game animals was maintained by deliberate systems of rotation in hunting and gathering, and defended by the family groups as a heritage from some remote time when the country had been given to their ancestors by the Creator. (pp. 258–259)

What Speck (1939) called "naked possession"[10] led to

the maintenance of a supply of animal and vegetable life, methods of insuring its propagation to provide sources of life for posterity, the permanent family residence within well-known and oftentimes blazed property boundaries, and resentment against trespass by the family groups surrounding them who possessed districts of their own. (p. 259)

Among the Indians of the western United States, where private land ownership was less common, exclusive, communal use rights for hunting, fishing, gathering, or agriculture were claimed (Steward, 1938, p. 254). Steward reports that among Paiute Indians of the Owens Valley "communal groups stayed within their district territory" (1934, p. 252) bounded by natural features such as mountains, ridges, and streams. Each distinct Apache "had its own hunting grounds and, except when pressed by starvation, was reluctant to encroach upon those of a neighbor. . . . Each local group had exclusive rights to certain farm sites and hunting localities, and each was headed by a chief who directed collective enterprises" (Basso, 1970, p. 5).

As with the Inuit, customs and norms regulated the harvest. There was a district headman who determined where and when to hunt based on his knowledge from the past. Throughout Indian culture, such headsmen were the "scientific managers," in many cases probably having better information about the resources than do their modern day counterparts.

Perhaps the best example of territorial fishing rights comes from the Pacific Northwest where Indians had well-established fishing sites along the Columbia River.[11] Indians recognized that fish wheels, weirs, and other fixed appliances at falls or shoals where the fish were naturally channeled were the simplest methods of harvesting fish that return from the ocean to spawn in freshwater streams. "The red man had studied carefully the habits and movements of the salmon and knew that the places to trap them were at the mouths of the tributaries and churning cascades and waterfalls" (Netboy, 1958, p. 11).

Their technology was so efficient that they could have depleted salmon stocks, but they realized the importance of allowing some of the spawning fish to escape upstream. Higgs quotes a Quileute Indian born about 1852: "When the Indians had obtained enough fish they would remove the weirs from the river in order that the fish they did not need could go upstream and lay their eggs so that there would be a supply of fish for future years" (1982, p. 59). In an important case regarding Indian fishing rights in the Pacific Northwest, the Boldt decision (named for Judge George Boldt) summarized historic Indian fishing rights:

> Generally, individual Indians had primary use rights in the territory where they resided and permissive use rights in the natal territory (if this was different) or in territories where they had consanguineal kin. Subject to such individual claims, most groups claimed autumn fishing use rights in the waters near to their winter villages. Spring and summer fishing areas were often more distantly located and often were shared with other groups from other villages. . . . Certain types [of fishing gear] required cooperative effort in their construction and/or handling. Weirs were classed as cooperative property but the component fishing stations on the weir were individually controlled. (*United States v. Washington,* 384 F. Supp. 312 [1974], 352–353)

Higgs notes that sites for "the fishing stands at the great Cleilo Falls of the Columbia, and the reef locations of the Lummi tribe in the northern Puget Sound . . . were heritable individual properties passed down from father to son" (1982, p. 59).

Unfortunately, the system of property rights in fishing sites developed by the Indians was ignored by the non-Indians entering the area in the nineteenth century. These non-Indians continually moved fishing operations closer and closer to the mouth of the Columbia River, taking as many fish as they could, until it was clear that the fishery would be destroyed. The government response was to shorten seasons and require fishermen to chase the fish in the open ocean. The result was what Higgs described as a "legally induced technical regress" (1982, p. 55). Unfortunately, the white man's law was "economically inferior to the property system originally established by the tribes" (Barsh, 1977, p. 23).

Personal Property

Though ownership of land and natural resources varied considerably depending on scarcity and improvements, personal property was nearly always privately owned and traded. Clothes, weapons, utensils, and housing were often owned by the women for whom they provided a way to accumulate personal wealth. For the Plains Indians, the tepee offers an example of private ownership. Women collected enough hides (usually between 8 and 20), tanned and scraped them, and prepared a great feast where the hides were sewn together by the participants.

Given the effort required to produce personal property, it was worth the while of the individual to specify and defend private property rights. Weeks or months could be spent collecting buffalo hides for tepees. Time was spent chipping arrow heads, constructing bows and arrows, and weaving baskets. To the extent that labor was necessary to convert raw materials into useful goods, the laborer owned the goods he or she produced.

> Water, seed, and hunting areas, minerals and salt deposits, etc., were freely utilized by anyone. But once work had been done upon the products of natural resources (mixed labor with them) they became the property of the person or family doing the work. Willow groves could be used by anyone, but baskets made of willows belonged to their makers. Wild seeds could be gathered by anyone, but once harvested, they belonged strictly to the family doing the task. (Steward, 1934, p. 253)

In cases where the resources themselves were scarce,

efforts to define and enforce personal rights also occurred. Stone from which arrowheads were chipped was obtained through long-distance trade and was personal property. Special wood for bows was also the object of trade, meaning that private ownership was necessary. In short, property rights were defined and enforced in accordance with the scarcity of the good in question.

Perhaps the best example of private ownership was the horse, which revolutionized transportation for Plains Indians, allowing them to live a life of abundance following the buffalo herds. A good horse was crucial to harvesting buffalo; it could be ridden into a stampeding herd so that arrows could be shot at close range. The horse became one of the Indian's most important sources of wealth. "A buffalo runner of known ability was worth several common riding horses or pack animals" (Ewers, 1958, p. 78). In Canada in the early 1800s, a buffalo horse could not be purchased with ten guns—a price far greater than any other tribal possession (Barsness, 1985, p. 61). Consider trader Charles Larpenteur's 1860 description of a wealthy Blackfoot man:

> It is a fine sight to see one of those big men among the Blackfeet, who has two or three lodges, five or six wives, twenty or thirty children, and fifty to a hundred horses; for his trade amounts to upward of $2,000 a year. (1898, p. 401)

Converting this amount to 1990 dollars, such a man had an annual income of approximately $500,000.

Given their value, horses were well cared for and closely guarded. Wissler states that "no system of branding was used, but each person knew the individualities of his horses so that he could recognize them" (1910, p. 97). Apparently, disputes over ownership were few, but if a horse was stolen, the offense was punishable by death. Perhaps more than any other asset, the horse reflects the extent to which Indian culture utilized the institution of private ownership.[12]

Getting the Incentives Right

In conclusion, it is useful to consider rules for group activities that reduced the incentive to shirk and provided a return on investment in both physical and human capital. For example, hunting skills required a considerable investment in time and equipment if the hunter was to be successful. Often "rabbits were hunted by a communal drive under the leadership of a secular rabbit chief. The officer was distinct from both the leader of the deer hunt and the antelope charmer" (Freed, 1960, p. 351). The nets into which the rabbits were driven, however, were privately owned and maintained. "The catch of these large drives was usually divided equally among those who participated, but sometimes a larger share was offered to the hunt's organizer and leader or to the owners of the nets" (Fowler, 1986, p. 82).[13]

For hunting larger game with bow and arrow, not only did the archer have to spend hours perfecting his shooting skills, but he had to chip the points for his arrows and construct his bow from costly materials capable of accurately launching the projectile. After the introduction of the horse, skilled riders and well-trained horses became the ingredients for success on a buffalo hunt. Under such circumstances, institutions arose to reward those willing to make the necessary investments. Indeed, the hunter was "entitled to keep the skin and some choice portion of the meat for his family" (Steward, 1938, p. 253). When the men had finished a hunt, they "located the buffalo they had killed by the marks on their arrows in the fallen beasts" (Ewers, 1969, p. 160). Disputes over whose arrow killed the buffalo were settled by the hunt leader. "Poor families which either were unable to borrow buffalo horses or possessed no able-bodied hunter in their lodges were forced to rely upon the charity of the wealthy for their buffalo meat" (p. 163). By following the hunt, "they could generally find successful hunters who would give them meat to carry home for their consumption," but the hunters "were loathe to give away the meat of fat cows. They generally preferred to give lean meat to the poor" (p. 162).

Owners of horses were also rewarded according to the value of their animals. It took strong, well-disciplined horses to run into a stampeding buffalo herd and keep up with the stronger buffalo. Four or five buffalo cows might be killed "on a single chase by the best Blackfoot marksman with the best horse under him. Most hunters rarely killed more than one or two buffalo at a chase. Men with inferior buffalo horses had to be satisfied with killing the slower running bulls" (Ewers, 1969, p. 159).

If an owner decided to loan his horse for a chase, there was the expectation of payment. Three Calf described to Ewers the arrangement his father made when loaning his horse. "There was no agreement in advance for any payment to be made to my father. If the man was selfish and offered my father no meat, the next time he wished to borrow horse, father told him, 'No'" (1969, p. 161). Because the chase was dangerous and a loaned horse might be injured, risk was taken into account in horse transactions. The responsible borrower who had taken reasonable precautions to prevent injury generally did not have to pay damages, but the irresponsible borrower was forced to replace the lost horse.

Faced with the reality of scarcity, Indians understood the importance of incentives and built their societies around institutions that encouraged good human and natural resource stewardship. The anthropological evidence suggests that Huffman's conclusion that "it is not entirely true that Native Americans knew nothing of ownership" (1992, p. 907) is most certainly an understatement. The lesson learned from Indians is that clearly specified property rights helped encourage conservation of scarce resources. A healthy dose of respect for Mother Nature may have reinforced Indian actions, but the tradition of efficient institutions that sanctioned irresponsible behavior and rewarded stewardship surely was an important component of Indian societies.

Notes

1. Group behavior may also be explained by genetic relations and survival of specific characteristics to the collective. See Dawkins (1976).

2. An example of this weakening can be found in small religious groups such as the Amish and the Hutterites where group size and outside social pressures make it more difficult to control individual action through religious codes.

3. The title for this section comes from Ellickson (1991).

4. For a complete account of the Chief Seattle myth, see Wilson (1992).

5. The lack of property rights to natural resources was due to the fact that natural resources in their "raw" state were not scarce; therefore it was not worth expending effort to define property rights to them. Eagle nests were an exception, probably because they were scarce and therefore demanded husbanding. Chapter 3 has more to say on this topic.

6. The Shoshone lifestyle can be contrasted with Indians in the Pacific Northwest who lived in close proximity to one another in a land of plenty. See Johnsen (1986).

7. For an extensive discussion of Hopi agriculture and land ownership, see Forde (1931).

8. See Kennard (1979, pp. 554–557) and Forde (1931) for details.

9. For a more complete discussion of property rights to piñon trees, see Lowie (1940).

10. This principle is similar to the Lockean proviso. The irony, however, is that when Locke first propounded his theory, he conspicuously ignored its application to Indian culture, proclaiming that America was in a state of nature before the white man arrived, just waiting for him to come and homestead it, to claim his share. See Chase (1986, pp. 110–111).

11. For a more complete discussion, see Higgs (1982).

12. Chapter 3 will examine the extent to which horses changed the constraints facing tribes and led to new institutional arrangements.

13. Though no anthropological evidence seems to be available to explain why organizers, leaders, or net owners might have received a larger share, it is likely that the differential reflected the

greater contribution that these people made to the hunt. This suggests that Indians were not necessarily egalitarian and that rewards for effort were based on the value of the individual's contribution.

Adaptation for Survival[1]

The variety of institutions that governed American Indians prior to European contact reflects the Indians' dynamic response to changing physical and man-made constraints. Indeed, "long before Darwin and Wallace brought biological evolution to the attention of the world in 1858, observers of the American Indian had recognized that evolution occurs in cultures" (Farb, 1968, p. 6). This evolution produced institutional arrangements as varied as any found in human history.

And just as Darwin's theory of evolution predicts that surviving species must change in response to ecological constraints, successful institutional change requires adaptation to new resource constraints.[2] According to Bailey (1992), the evolution of culture and institutions in aboriginal societies often occurred

at the margin of subsistence. In more developed societies, departures from optimality mean lower living standards and lower growth rates—luxuries these societies can afford. By contrast, in societies near the margin of subsistence, with populations under Malthusian control, such departures had harsher ef-

> fects.... Unsound rights structures generally implied lower population size and, perhaps, the disappearance of the society. (p. 183)

Bailey no doubt overstates the extent to which institutions of these societies were driven by Malthusian forces. Indeed, many American Indians enjoyed a bounty from nature. Nonetheless, Bailey's emphasis on evolution is appropriate as even the most prosperous societies face changing time and resource constraints. This evolutionary response to these changes need not have been motivated by conscious individual or group efforts to maximize wealth. Instead, trial and error accompanied by replication could generate "approximately optimal" institutions. Alchian (1950) relates the approaches of the biologist and the economist:

> Like the biologist, the economist predicts the effects of environmental changes on the surviving class of living organisms; the economist need not assume that each participant is aware of, or acts according to, his cost and demand situation. These are concepts for the economist's use and not necessarily for the individual participant's, who may have other analytic or customary devices. (p. 221)

Simply put, people produce institutions just as they produce other goods and services; that is, institutions evolve in response to changes in costs and benefits. In his seminal article on the evolution of property rights, Demsetz argued that "the emergence of new property takes place in response to the desires of the interacting persons for adjustment to new benefit-cost possibilities" (1967, p. 350). For some animal species like the beaver, increased scarcity made it economical for Indians to establish property institutions that encouraged a sustained yield. For other species, such as the buffalo, however, the costs of establishing ownership remained prohibitive throughout the nineteenth century (see Lueck, 1993).

To the extent that institutional change is gradual and continuous, occurring at a local level where those making the changes are directly affected, the change is more likely to be wealth enhancing. As with biological evolution, such institutional change takes advantage of time and place specific conditions that signal opportunities for increasing wealth. Even in cases where the impetus for changes are discontinuous, as with the introduction of the horse into Indian culture, the institutional response was quick and effective. Trenholm and Carley (1964) describe the Shoshone's transition to the Plains:

> While the Indians retained many of their legends and customs, they were receptive to their new environment and to the way of life of enemy tribes whose background was far different from their own. Resistance was lacking since Plains culture was not forced upon them, and the change was gradual, if never complete. In fact, these Basin aborigines were unaware that they were adjusting to their surroundings sufficiently to be called Plains Shoshonis. (p. vii)

Institutional change encompasses a gamut of cultural elements including religious beliefs, social norms, codes of conduct, private contracts, and formal law. In this chapter, I will highlight the richness of Indian institutions and institutional changes in these areas. Though the coverage is not exhaustive, it illustrates the diversity of norms, customs, and property rights found among American aboriginals.

Explaining Institutional Change

Explanations of the evolution of property rights have emphasized the important role of relative prices.[3] As North puts it, "fundamental changes in relative prices are the most important source of that change," because "relative price changes alter the incentives of individuals in human interaction" (1990, p. 84). Such heavy emphasis on relative prices may seem inappropriate for aboriginal societies, but Smith notes that even prehistoric humans were able "to adapt to changes in their environment by substituting new types of capital, labor and knowledge for old, and by fabricating new products when effort prices were altered by the environment or by new learning" (1992, pp. 5–6).

Of course, ideology can provide another potential source of institutional change, and this has received more attention in the case of aboriginal societies. "Changing relative prices are filtered through preexisting mental constructs that shape our understanding of those price changes. Clearly ideas, and the way they take hold, play a role here" (North, 1990, p. 85). In this process "cultural elements are in a continual process of interaction: new syntheses and combinations are constantly being produced. But whether or not the new combinations survive in a human group depends on whether or not they work in the existing cultural context. An invention or new combination can be successful only if all of the elements necessary for the recombination are present in the culture" (Farb, 1968, p. 10).

Because Indians generally lacked strong, central political organizations, most of their institutional change occurred at a decentralized level. Hence, the creation, development, and ruin of institutions hinged mostly on individual decisions. This is not to say, however, that collective action was absent in Indian institutional change. Especially as the horse increased the territorial range of Indian groups, interaction became less personal and scale economies in warfare increased. This meant that formal tribal institutions evolved to govern relations in a more heterogeneous population and to organize warfare. Moreover, as I will show in Chapter 5, contact with the white man and his central government made institutional change more a function of endogenous collective choices as Indians first combined forces in war and later were relegated to reservations under centralized tribal governments.[4] Most of this chapter, however, focuses on individual or small group adaptation.

Explaining the evolution of Indian institutions has been largely the domain of anthropologists[5] for whom the question of private ownership of land among aboriginals has held a particular fascination. "It has been one of the intellectual battlegrounds in the attempt to assess the 'true nature' of man unconstrained by the 'artificialities' of civilization" (Demsetz, 1967, p. 351). Through this debate, anthropologists became keenly aware of institutional change among North American Indians. For example, Steward observed that "band ownership of food territories obviously originated somewhere for good reasons. Its repeated occurrence among widely separated groups in different parts of the world suggests that under certain conditions it has developed very readily" (1941, p. 255).

But some anthropologists have tended to shun the explanatory power of economic models, contending that "primitive economy is different from market industrialism not in degree but in kind. The absence of machine technology, pervasive market organization, and all-purpose money, plus the fact that economic transactions cannot be understood apart from social obligation, create . . . a non-Euclidean universe to which Western economic theory cannot be fruitfully applied" (Dalton, 1961, p. 20).

Recently, however, some economists have taken a keener interest in the evolution of aboriginal institutions and fruitfully applied their models.[6] Posner's theory of primitive society emphasized that "many of the distinctive institutions of primitive society, including gift giving and reciprocal exchange, customary prices, polygamy and bridesprice, the size of kinship groups, and the value placed on certain personality traits, such as generosity and touchiness, can be explained as adaptations to uncertainty or high information costs" (1980, p. 4). To this list of distinctive features we must add common property, which often typified Indian property institutions.[7] Aboriginal circumstances that made common property institutions an optimal system "generally included a small population when compared to a modern nation state, so that the enforcement of various behavioral norms through social pressure was much easier. For this and other technological reasons, optimal rights structures in aboriginal societies could include more common property and group enterprises and fewer disjoint [sic] individual rights" (Bailey, 1992, p. 184).

Three factors condition the choice between disjointed individual activities and rights and group enterprises.[8] First, scale economies were determined by a variety of forces including technology, geography, and biology. For example, without horses, hunting buffalo in the vicinity of cliffs encouraged coordinated hunting because it would "produce better total results for the group than would an individual's solitary tracking" (Bailey, 1992, p. 188).[9]

Second, communal organizations allowed a way for subsistence societies to share risk in the face of variability within a hunting season due to game location and variability across seasons due to weather, biological cycles, and so on. Because the primitive technology made it costly to "self-insure" against this variability by storing food, communal arrangements for sharing scarce food supplies reduced individual risk.

Third, the gains from scale economies available from group action had to be traded off against the potential for shirking by individual members of the collective. This point has been emphasized in modern political economy (see especially Cheung, 1983; Coase, 1937) in terms of the costs of measuring and monitoring performance between contracting parties. For the firm, potential shirking by workers is overcome by hiring managers to oversee production. Monitoring managers, however, is more difficult. Alchian and Demsetz (1972) point out that the modern firm overcomes this problem by assigning to the firm's owner a claim on the residual profit thereby giving him a stake in the monitoring process. In social groups, however, such owner-residual claimants are not always well identified. Of course, in small, closely knit societies, shirking is limited because the costs of shirking are much more concentrated and because culture, religion, and customs constrain individual behavior. When these three points are combined with the simple point that institutions change with relative prices, it is easy to understand why American Indian societies were so dynamic, especially after the arrival of the horse.

Property Rights to Wildlife

Contact with Europeans through fur trading dramatically changed the value of fur bearing animals and the incentive to establish rules that would prevent animal populations from being overexploited. In the absence of any rules governing animal harvest, self-interested individuals would have an in-centive to take animals without regard for the impact on the future productivity of the resource. The "tragedy of the commons" would result with completely open access to the resource because an individual's decision to leave an animal to grow and reproduce would be unsuccessful; any animal not harvested would be available to the next person with access to the commons.[10] Indians successfully avoided this tragedy by developing rules limiting access to the commons, thereby encouraging resource stewardship.

The rules that evolved governing beaver trapping in the

Northeast illustrate how property rights evolved. Before trade, Indians hunted the beaver primarily for food and for the small number of furs required by the hunter's family. The potential for overexploitation existed, but demands on the resource were not sufficient to warrant investments to refine the property rights structure. There were no landowning units or family hunting territories; "instead all resources were 'free goods'" (Rogers & Leacock, 1981, p. 181).

Once trade was established, however, the price of furs rose, increasing hunting pressures and changing the incentive to invest in property rights. "With the emergence of a full-fledged trapping economy, usufructuary rights to trap in specific territories became established" (Rogers & Leacock, 1981, p. 181). Early in the eighteenth century Leacock described

> clear evidence that territorial hunting and trapping arrangements by individual families were developing in the area around Quebec. . . . The earliest references to such arrangements in the region indicates a purely temporary allotment of hunting territories. They [Algonquians and Iroquois] divide themselves into several small bands in order to hunt more efficiently. It was their custom . . . to appropriate pieces of land about two leagues square for each group to hunt exclusively. (quoted in Demsetz, 1967, p. 352)

Leacock quotes an anonymous account from 1723 that notes that Indians marked "off the hunting ground selected by them by blazing the trees with their crests so that they may never encroach on each other. . . . By the middle of the century these allotted territories were relatively stabilized" (quoted in Demsetz, 1967, p. 352). Similarly, the Northern Ojibwa "evolved a concept of vaguely demarcated 'hunting territories'. . . . At first, only beaver lodges were marked to denote 'ownership' of the beaver therein, but in time territorial boundaries were established for each hunting-trapping group. Within each territory the group had exclusive rights to the fur resources but not to other resources or to the land itself" (Rogers & Taylor, 1981, p. 236). The resulting property rights structure reflected the fact that it was the fur resource and not the land that was scarce.

The Kolchan and Koyukon of Alaska were also influenced

by the fur trade. The Kolchan became less nomadic and established property rights for a variety of animal resources. Prior to the fur trade, the Kolchan had been more nomadic, due to the low predictability of prey and plant locations. With trade, however, "they became more sedentary and permanent villages were established. As the land gained an economic value, band ownership of trapping areas weakened in favor of family rights" (Hosley, 1981, p. 621). For the Koyukon, these family rights extended beyond beaver houses to muskrat swamps, fishing locations, bear hibernation holes, berrying grounds, some bird hunting territories, and even to certain big game territories where fences were built (Clark, 1981, p. 585).

Interestingly, in keeping with Posner's hypothesis that common property rights provided an insurance mechanism for sharing risk, it was generally the case that "a starving Indian could kill and eat another's beaver if he left the fur and the tail" (Leacock quoted in Demsetz, 1967, p. 352).[11] "Trespass with the intent of securing furs or other products for trade," on the other hand, "was resented and threatened with punishment through shamanistic performances" (Rogers & Leacock, 1981, p. 181).

It is important to note that "there is no evidence that the bands ever acted as political units to arbitrate disputes regarding their boundaries or those of their component hunting groups; instead the hunting groups that were involved apparently arranged a settlement among themselves" (Rogers & Leacock, 1981, p. 181). In other words, the property rights that evolved in response to the fur trade did so spontaneously rather than through governmental fiat. They were enforced through kinship ties and common cultural traditions. The evolution of property rights in this setting of small groups as opposed to rules handed down from central governments was more likely to approach "approximate optimality" (see Bailey, 1992) because the actors were aware of the resource scarcities and had a stake in enforcing rules governing harvest. The threat of force was necessary to enforce property rights, but kinship, cultural norms, and customs minimized violence.

The evolution of property rights to trapping territories in the Northeast contrasts sharply with the Indian experience on the Great Plains. The Shoshone wandered over vast areas in search of prey and plants without establishing property rights to territories or animals. Two factors explain the absence of property rights (see Demsetz, 1967, p. 353). First, the commercial value of fur and hides less transportation costs was low until the coming of the railroad. Second, the animals of the Plains were primarily grazing animals that wandered over vast areas, making it difficult to establish private hunting territories or to prevent the animals from moving to other territories. The simple point is that given the costs of establishing property rights on the Plains, the potential tragedy of the commons "was just not worth taking into account" (Demsetz, 1967, p. 353). Even after buffalo hides became more valuable as a result of the white man's demand, the costs of specifying property rights remained prohibitive, contributing to the decimation of herds.

The Horse Culture

> The horse has come. Almost overnight, it seems, he has captured the west; and by his coming the west has been awakened, transformed. It was one of the most dramatic and one of the most momentous transformations that ever took place in any land under the sun. The bare facts of the coming of the horse and the transformation thus wrought constitute the greatest animal epic ever enacted in the world. (Sass, 1936, p. 5)

The arrival of the horse dramatically altered the way of life for many Indian tribes, especially those on the Plains, necessitating that they adopt many institutional changes if they were to survive. Especially evident were changes in the size of the socioeconomic group, change in the locus of leadership for various group activities, and increased trade between tribes.

Pre-Equestrian Life

Prior to arrival of the Spanish horse, the life of the Indians inhabiting the Great Plains was considerably different. Though far from sedentary, mobility was much more limited as the dog provided the major form of transportation of household goods. Except for some Indians, especially those in the middle and upper Missouri River drainage who lived relatively sedentary, horticultural lives,[12] most tribes of the Plains depended on the buffalo as a mainstay in their diet and for household commodities. Given the migratory nature of the buffalo, these Indians were necessarily nomadic, but given their dependence on the dog for transportation, their possessions were fewer, their lodges were smaller (usually five or six buffalo skins and shorter poles), and the distances traveled were shorter (see Ewers, 1968, p. 8).

When the pre-equestrian Indian did encounter buffalo, hunting techniques were generally confined to one of two methods, the surround or the drive. As the name suggests, the surround required that the buffalo be encircled in a make-shift fence. A group of swift-footed men would rouse the herd and drive it toward the fence while others would stand alongside the drive route and close in behind the herd. Once surrounded, the buffalo herd would run in a circle while hunters slaughtered them with arrows. A more spontaneous, though less successful, surround might do away with the fence altogether, and merely use Indians waving buffalo robes or arms to create the illusion of an obstacle.[13]

The alternative to the surround was the pedestrian drive, which was truly the maximalist form of pedestrian hunting. Using the drive promised the wholesale slaughter of an entire herd but at a great expense of planning, labor, coordination, and care. The drive usually involved herding the buffalo into a permanent man-made pound called a piskun or, better yet, stampeding the herd over a cliff. Because the buffalo had to be near a piskun or cliff to have a successful drive, Indians had to move with the herds. Therefore, in the spring when "the buffalo would move down to the more flat prairie country away from the pis'kuns . . . the Blackfeet would also move away. As winter drew near, the buffalo would again move up close to the mountains, and the Indians as food began to become scarce, would follow them toward the pis'kuns" (Grinnell, 1962, p. 234).

Both the surround and the drive required careful coordination by a hunt leader who had a great deal of knowledge about buffalo and who had authority over the hunters.[14] This leader would appoint guards "who prevented the disruption of the communal effort by attempts to hunt alone in advance of the village. These guards punished offenders through destruction of their property 'without the man or woman saying a word'" (Ewers, 1969, p. 303). This authority generally did not extend to other individual or group activities, so the hunt chief did not represent a form of tribal government except during the hunt itself.

As long as buffalo were in the area near the piskun, it was worth undertaking the coordination costs because the pedestrian Indians were rewarded with significant economies of scale and abundant quantities of meat.[15] When drives required moving the animals to the location of the trap or cliff, the herd would be led slowly into drive lines made of stones, buffalo chips, or any other available material. The herd was funnelled toward the trap as Indians stood at the sidelines beating their robes to prevent the buffalo from testing the durability of the drive lines. To prevent the herd from escaping, many people were needed along the lines, especially as the buffalo approached the trap or cliff.

Families could pursue buffalo on their own using the pedestrian stalk, but this technique was not as productive as group efforts except under special conditions. For example, during the winter when the buffalo were mired in deep snowdrifts the pedestrian hunter could be quite successful (Ewers, 1958, p. 84). After a warm day or two of thawing and then refreezing, the snow surface might become hard enough to support a man on snowshoes but collapse under the buffalo's hooves. The disparity in ground speed would then be narrowed, and the Indians with snowshoes could dart across the snow's surface to great advantage. Sometimes the buffalo could be run down and killed with a dagger or spear (see Arthur, 1975, p. 64; Hornaday, 1889, p. 423).[16] It was also possible to stalk buffalo near water holes, river crossings, and salt licks.

Anthropological data show that the optimal band size for pedestrian drives was between 100 and 300 people.[17] White writes: "The most comfortable size of a band was usually felt to be about 100–150 persons, but it was often much smaller. When it began to swell in size, and approach the 200 mark, the problem of feeding it became serious, and the usual solution was fission" (1979, p. 55). Barsness claims that a permanent band of 150 people may have been the optimal number of participants in a buffalo drive (1985, p. 38). When a group got larger than this, it would peaceably divide, apparently because the coordination costs rose significantly (see Wissler, 1966, ch.

18). When there were not sufficient buffalo in the area of the trap or cliff, it made little sense to live together in these large bands. During the summer when buffalo migrated to the green grass of the open plains, Indian bands dispersed into smaller groups.

When buffalo were plentiful in the area of the piskun, meat was abundant. Drives were especially productive in the autumn when the bulls had separated themselves and buffalo were more likely to be moving off the open plains. Meat was so plentiful after a successful drive that consumption was high: "It was not unusual for a man to consume eight or ten pounds of it in a day" (Ewers, 1968, p. 170). The Blackfeet were so successful at procuring large quantities of buffalo using the drive technique that they could supply the white traders with meat and pemmican while providing for their own needs during the lean winter months (see Henry & Thompson, 1965, 2, pp. 530, 723–725).

Abundance also resulted in waste, because the number of buffalo killed in a drive could not be easily controlled. Especially when the number of workers who could butcher was small compared to the kill and when the kill site was far from the main camp, light butchering was common—only the tongues and choicest cuts of meat were taken. Barsness guesses that after a successful drive "perhaps only fifty percent of the dead animals became human food: Conspicuous Consumption" (1985, pp. 47–48). Often so much meat was left rotting at the base of a buffalo jump cliff that the stench could last for months making it impossible to drive any buffalo to that location.

Pre-equestrian Plains Indians lived together in relatively large bands to reap the benefits of scale economies. Their hunting techniques required strong hunt chiefs supported by tribal police societies that enforced the rules of the hunt, but there was little other evidence of governmental authority and certainly nothing that resembled tribal government. When the collective hunting seasons ended, the bands dispersed into family and clan units where authority resided with the head of the household and survival depended on individual rather than collective enterprise.

Post-Equestrian Institutions

The horse substantially changed life for many Indian tribes by reducing transportation costs and increasing mobility. "The immediate effect upon the Indians of the acquisition of a few Spanish horses by trade or theft was to discourage what little agricultural work they did, and cause them to rely upon the buffalo more than ever before. . . . With the horse they roamed for miles, encroached upon others' hunting grounds, went to war, and otherwise became marauders of the plains" (Wyman, 1945, p. 70).[18]

> As life on the Plains became more inviting with the use of horses, more tribes moved out there, the Sioux and Cheyennes, and Araphahos from the east, the Comanches and Kiowas from the west. Some abandoned their agriculture entirely and based their economy on buffalo herds—"We lost the corn," say the Cheyennes. Others like the Osages maintained their fixed residences, where they planted their crops, rode out to the Plains for their supply of meat, and returned to harvest their corn and settle down for the winter. (Debo, 1970, p. 15)

The horse also changed the Indian's housing, in some cases from permanent lodges to tepees and in many cases to larger tepees, now a symbol of Plains life. In the "dog days" when canines were used for transportation, Indian tepees were smaller, averaging five or six hides and measuring approximately 12 feet in diameter. As Ewers notes, "the necessity of dragging the lodgepoles, which increased in length and weight with the size of the lodge, must have encouraged the use of small lodges in the years before horses were available for pole dragging services" (1955, p. 307). With the horse the average size of tepees increased because a horse could drag an 18 or 20 foot diameter tepee and its poles. A complete post-equestrian tepee weighed more than 500 pounds and required three horses to transport (Ewers, 1969, p. 134). "Once the horse was introduced, the tepee became larger (the horse could carry the longer poles required of a larger tepee) and its territory expanded. The tepee spread so far because there was always a ready supply of buffalo skins for the cover and because it could be used in just about any terrain or climate" (Faegre, 1979, p. 152).

The size of socioeconomic groups and seasonal economic

patterns shifted dramatically with adaptation to the horse culture. Acquisition of the horse reduced the scale economies in hunting, making the socioeconomic group smaller. Though the transition costs to switch from more sedentary agriculture to nomadic hunting must have been great, the ethnohistorical record indicates that some tribes undertook these costs and became fully nomadic in two or three generations.[19] On horseback, individuals could more easily track and kill game using either the mounted surround or the mounted chase. Using the surround, mounted horsemen could charge hopeless buffalo, dispatching the creatures with arrows. Though the buffalo might charge and gore a hunter's mount and cause some mayhem, a surround party of 80 to 100 people could "kill from 100 to 500 buffalo in the course of an hour" (Catlin, 1965, 1, pp. 199–200). But such large hunts required coordination and therefore were the exception rather than the norm.

Even the smallest social unit could live independently and provide for itself. Hence, communal hunting declined with the improved ability for individuals or small groups to follow and harvest game (see Ewers, 1969, p. 165) and thereby reduced the need for communal insurance schemes. The horse made it possible for hunters to bring the kill site to the buffalo rather than bringing the buffalo to the kill site.

> It was the chase on horseback that fully exploited the horse's ability to run faster than the swiftest buffalo. This new hunting technique was more efficient and adaptable than any method previously employed. Not only did it require a fraction of the time and energy but it was less dangerous and more certain of success than other methods. It could be employed by a single hunter. Within a few minutes a skilled hunter, mounted on a fleet, intelligent, buffalo horse could kill at close range enough buffalo to supply his family with meat for months. (Ewers, 1969, p. 305)

With this form of hunting, the role of the hunt chief declined as the importance of a skilled horseman with a trusty buffalo horse rose, and this change was reflected in the compensation schemes. In the pedestrian communal hunt where everyone contributed approximately equally to productivity, the product was distributed evenly among the hunters, with some accord given to the number of dependents. The decoyer or poundmaster might be allotted a differential amount of meat due to the higher risks or special skills and everyone would pass on a certain portion—often the tongues—to the hunt leader (see Denig, 1930, p. 533; Henry & Thompson, 1965, p. 520).

In the horse culture, however, it was the individuals who could ride and shoot arrows and owned buffalo horses who received the lion's share. Each buffalo belonged to the mounted horseman who launched the lethal arrow, which was clearly marked. Poor people (that is, those without a strong buffalo horse) would take their dogs or common horses to help in the butchering and transport of the meat and hides. In exchange for their services, the hunter would give them some of the lean meat and less choice cuts (Ewers 1969, p. 162). But a hunter could gain stature by increasing the number of his dependents, since a larger number of dependents would give the hunter a more powerful voice in the community.

Groups also dispersed because the horse required adequate pasturage and water, necessitating more frequent movements of camp (Lowie, 1982, p. 42). With a Blackfoot lodge averaging 15 horses and a Cayuse lodge averaging 15 to 20 horses, it is easy to see why large bands could face forage shortages (Farnham, 1843, p. 82).

If the horse reduced economies of scale in hunting and hence the need for centralized hunting institutions, it increased the need for military institutions and their inherent scale economies. "It was . . . leisure time, the rise of the pony as a measure of wealth, and the infringement upon one another's buffalo range that was a cause of intertribal war" (Wyman, 1945, p. 74). Increased mobility brought more conflict between tribes for larger hunting territories and more raids to steal horses. To organize for intertribal warfare, new, more centralized political structures evolved to capture the scale economies. Shimkin describes this transition for the Eastern Shoshone: "With the acquisition of horses came . . . widespread raiding throughout the Plains, 1700–1780. In this period, it is certain that strong chiefly leadership and considerable protocol and sumptuary rights prevailed" (1986, p. 309). Prior to the horse, there was likely less intertribal warfare. For the Blackfoot, one of the fiercest Plains tribes, "traditions claim that the Shoshoni were their only enemies in pre-horse times" (Ewers, 1969, p. 172). After acquisition of the horse, however, intertribal warfare was more common. "Throughout the century prior to 1885, peace between the Blackfoot tribes and their neighbors (other than Sarsi and Gros Ventres) was the exception, war the rule. Peaceful periods were brief interludes between hostilities" (Ewers, 1969, p. 175).

The enhanced mobility meant that tribes would more frequently encounter one another and potentially fight over common herds of buffalo. The heightened danger of encroachment by other tribes, the greater dependence on the buffalo, and the ability to patrol and protect an area thanks to the horse made the declaration of private tribal hunting grounds ubiquitous. Tribes drew boundary lines and signed treaties to defend them; if no clear topographic features existed to delineate the boundary, boulders wrapped in buffalo hides were substituted (Barsness, 1985, p. 53).

On the heels of intertribal warfare came conflicts with whites (see Chapter 4) and another pressure for institutional change to accommodate warfare. During the nineteenth century, institutions with strong tribal chiefs evolved for organizing warriors. In many cases, tribes were totally unprepared for these political changes; "The institution of the band chief was novel and hence provided opportunity for influential personalities to assert themselves" (Steward, 1938, p. 249). The horse and the accompanying warfare transformed the organization of Plains Indian tribes into political bands that, "like subsistence areas, interlocked in all directions. . . . Previously independent villages, now traveling with horses, united into military bands under high commands" (p. 248).[20]

Because the horse had such profound impacts on Indian life, it is not surprising that ownership of horses became a symbol of wealth and prestige. As discussed in Chapter 2, horses were always considered personal property with full rights of inheritance and trade, and the number of horses owned by tribal members could mean the difference between survival or conquest. Schultz remarked of the Blackfoot in the 1870s that "horses were the tribal wealth, and one who owned a large herd of them held a position only to be compared to that of our multi-millionaires. These were individuals who owned from one hundred to three and four hundred" (1907, p. 152).

With property rights in horses secure and good buffalo horses so valuable, groups became "noted for their attention to and skill in breeding horses" (Ewers, 1969, p. 22). This was especially true of Indians who "lived west of the Rockies where they were relatively immune from horse raids of the Plains Indians and where winters were milder and forage more plentiful than on the northern Plains" (p. 22). Under private ownership, the buffalo horse was treated with obsequious care. The hunter often rode a common horse to the locale of the chase to save the buffalo horse's energy. Meat and hides were rarely packed on a prized buffalo horse. Buffalo horses were kept apart from the other less valuable horses and close to the tepee where they could be protected from raiders. The horse would be cleaned of sweat and even rubbed down by a wife after a hard chase. And, when there was little forage, grass would be pulled for the prize horses or cottonwood bark peeled and fed by hand.[21]

The increased mobility afforded by the horse also increased the potential for trade among Indians. Different resource endowments such as materials for constructing bows and arrow points provided the potential for gains from trade even in pre-equestrian times, but pre-equestrian transport costs made it more difficult to realize these gains. Trade was not new to Indians, but with the coming of the horse trade was made easier. Ewers (1968) describes the complexity of Indian trade before Lewis and Clark:

> Not only did the Assiniboins and Crees trade with the Mandan-Hidatsas, but they also traded with the English of the Hudson's Bay and North West companies. . . . The Crows traveled to a trading rendezvous in the west with the Shoshonis, Flatheads, and Nez Perces, and the Shoshonis in turn traded, through the Utes west of the Rockies, with the Spaniards of New Mexico. The Cheyenne, Arapaho, Kiowa, Kiowa-Apache, and Comanche tribes not only traded with both the Mandans and the Arikaras but they also traveled to the Spanish settlements of the Southwest by way of the western high plains. The Tetons were

accustomed to meet other Dakota groups each spring
at a great rendezvous on the James River where they
received some of the goods supplied to the Sissetons
and Yanktons by North West Company traders. (p. 17)

The large profits from intertribal trade "encouraged individual
Indians who came into possession of desirable horses or guns
to furnish them to foreign tribesmen rather than to men of their
own tribes who lacked these valuable assets" (Ewers, 1968, p.
28). In addition to horses, weapons, tools, utensils, and food
were common trade items that were often retraded "at a hand-
some profit" (p. 28). Not only did western Indians trade among
themselves but they also successfully competed with white
traders for a share of the profits. "Jean-Baptiste Truteau, in
1795, found that the prices he was allowed to pay would not
permit him to compete successfully with the Teton Dakotas for
the beaver trade of the Arikaras" (Ewers, 1968, p. 30).[22]

Conclusion

The history of American Indians shows how readily they
adapted to different physical, economic, and social environments by changing the institutions that governed human relations. In most cases the institutional changes were marginal
adaptations, but in the case of the horse they were more
discontinuous. Indeed, it is remarkable how completely the
horse had transformed Plains Indian life by the middle of the
nineteenth century. While the nomadic horseman is an accepted symbol of the Indian life encountered by the first white
men on the western frontier, the horse and its accompanying
technology and institutions were relatively new to Indians. Had
the whites arrived a few decades earlier, they would have found
less mobile groups well organized for hunting but less well
organized for dealing with outsiders. As the horse increased the
potential for trade and conflict among Indians, it also better
prepared them for trading and warring with whites. In fact,
had the Indians not developed their military institutions in
response to the demands of intertribal warfare, it is problematic whether they could have resisted the onslaught of whites
as long as they did.

Left to their own devices, Indians can and have changed their institutions when they needed to do so. To understand the process of this change, the supporting structures peculiar to Indian life must be considered. Customs, traditions, and ideology played a vital role in the eighteenth- and nineteenth-century adaptations, but they were supplanted with centralized bureaucratic controls directed from Washington. Radical changes in the formal rules are usually the result of conquest or revolution (see North, 1990, p. 89) and therefore are substituted for spontaneous, self-determined institutional evolution. Given the radical, exogenous institutional changes that came to Indians after the middle of the nineteenth century, it should not be surprising that Indians have had to struggle to find an institutional environment where there is the "possibility of independence and autonomous political participation" (Barsh, 1987, p. 89).

Notes

1. Parts of this chapter were adapted from papers written by Claire Morgan and Steven LaCombe when they were fellows at the Political Economy Research Center, Bozeman, MT. Therefore, I owe them a special debt of gratitude for their contributions.

2. See Alchian (1950) for a discussion of the evolution and survival of successful institutional arrangements.

3. See especially Demsetz (1967) and Anderson and Hill (1975).

4. As tribes began to interface with one another and with federal bureaucracies, discontinuous institutional change became more prevalent. For example, the Indian Reorganization Act of 1934 required that tribes adopt constitutions that often were incongruous with traditional institutions.

5. Notable exceptions by economists who have written on this subject include Demsetz (1967), Posner (1980), Smith (1992), and Bailey (1992).

6. See Anderson (1992) for examples of this interest.

7. For additional emphasis on this point outside the American Indian context, see Anderson and Simmons (1993), Bromley (1992), and Ostrum (1990).

8. Bailey (1992, p. 187) lists five attributes of resources or technology that favor communal property rights. These are condensed into three categories here.

9. This point dovetails with Posner's information cost theory.

10. For the classic discussion of "the tragedy of the commons," see Hardin (1968).

11. Rogers and Leacock state that along with usufructuary rights came "the distinction between resources used for group needs and those that were sold or traded to Europeans. The former remained available to anyone, while the latter become the property of the hunting group or individual on whose territory they occurred" (1981, p. 181).

12. Even these tribes, however, spent part of the year pursuing the buffalo. See Ewers (1969, p. 152).

13. For an excellent discussion of the use of the drive and surround, see Ewers (1968, pp. 157–168).

14. For an excellent discussion of this method, see Branch (1962, pp. 35–40).

15. Of course, groups would try to economize on labor. The Crow, for example, burned incense along the drive lines to repel escaping animals. This allowed the Crow to concentrate their personnel at the very end of the drive, where stones would be stacked higher and closer together to provide greater protection for the braves. Fire also could be used to direct the buffalo herds if the group was shorthanded. See Medicine Crow (1978).

16. Even after the arrival of the horse, deep snows might preclude its use, thus necessitating the footed stalk in equestrian times (Arthur, 1975, p. 69).

17. The literature generally does not differentiate the community size for Plains Indians from other North American groups. White (1979, p. 76) gives the inclusive figure of 100 to 300 persons for the historic period. Wissler, however, writes: "An Indian community rarely consisted of more than a hundred persons of all ages" (1966, p. 261). Also see Ewers (1969, p. 303) and Henry and Thompson (1965, 2, p. 723).

18. Also see Baden, Stroup, and Thurman (1981) for an excellent discussion of Indian responses to relative prices.

19. For example, see Mulloy (1958, p. 215) and Grinnell (1972, p. 13).

20. It should be noted that these warfare institutions evolved out of necessity and disappeared when the Indians were subjugated by the whites. "The office and its duties, having no precedence in native institutions and concerning principally warfare negotiations with the white man, were limited in scope and duration. They survived too briefly to have won general respect and support. When the wars ceased, the need for organization largely vanished and the chiefs lost authority" (Steward, 1938, p. 249).

21. For details of the treatment of buffalo horses, see Ewers (1958, p. 78) and Barsness (1985, pp. 59–60).

22. For a discussion of the extensive trading network that formed see Albers (1993).

CHAPTER 4

The Political Economy of Indian-White Relations[1]

On March 27, 1792, Thomas Jefferson wrote to David Campbell:

> I hope too that your admonitions against encroachments on the Indian lands will have a beneficial effect—the U.S. finds an Indian war too serious a thing, to risk incurring one merely to gratify a few intruders with settlements which are to cost the other inhabitants of the U.S. a thousand times their value in taxes for carrying on the war they produce. I am satisfied it will ever be preferred to send armed force and make war against the intruders [the white settlers] as being more just & less expensive. (quoted in Prucha, 1962, p. 139)

The history of Indian-white relations is often portrayed as one in which whites ran roughshod over the rights of Indians. As Hughes put it, "from beginning to end primary title was deemed to come by right of conquest, Indian title being inferior in the views of the crown [and] the settlers" (1976, p. 35). Historian Don Russell characterizes the conventional tale as one long episode of "'massacre,' 'extermination,' and 'annihilation,' both 'utter' and 'complete'" recounted "with overtones of racism, genocide, and other shibboleths" (1973, p. 42). This portrayal of violence is certainly substantiated by the late nineteenth century experience with Custer's Last Stand, Chief Joseph's attempted escape to Canada, and the massacre at Wounded Knee.

But armed conflict did not always dominate Indian-white relations. The first Pilgrim Thanksgiving occurred in a setting of peaceful, mutually beneficial relations. During colonial times and during the early years of the republic, the federal government of the whites tried to negotiate with Indians over conflicting land claims, believing that white land claims were "unjustified and illegal if the prior rights of the Indian were not recognized. Full title was in the Indian . . . from whom alone a valid title could be derived" (Washburn, 1971, p. 41). More pragmatically, as Thomas Jefferson suggested in his letter to David Campbell, there was a concern that intruding on Indian lands would mean incurring unnecessary costs to defend white territory.

Table 4.1 shows the number of battles and treaties between Indians and whites for the period from 1790 to 1897. At

TABLE 4.1 Indian-White Battles and Treaties, 1790 to 1897

Year	Battles	Treaties
1790–1799	7	10
1800–1809	0	30
1810–1819	33	35
1820–1829	1	51
1830–1839	63	84
1840–1849	53	18
1850–1859	190	58
1860–1869	786	61
1870–1879	530	0
1880–1889	131	0
1890–1897	13	0

Source: Anderson and McChesney (1994).

the end of the eighteenth and for the first four decades of the nineteenth century, peacefully negotiated treaties significantly outnumbered battles. But something changed at mid-century to bring on relatively more bloody conflicts. In this chapter, I will explain this shift and its consequences in terms of the political economy of dispute resolution.

To Raid or Trade

In *The Rise of the West*, William McNeill states that "when it was no longer safe to seize valuables by main force, trade offered an alternative way of getting possessions. . . . Oscillation between raiding and trading has certainly occurred repeatedly in history" (1963, p. 454). To explain this oscillation, consider the process of dispute resolution. Before a dispute exists, harm must be done. Thereafter the harmed party must decide if the harm is sufficiently serious to warrant asserting a claim against the perpetrator. Once a claim is asserted, the parties can negotiate a settlement or do battle in court or on the battlefield.[2]

It should be noted, however, that disputants might be battling over vastly different land uses and hence different values. For the Plains Indians, land use was not at all intensive, making the value per acre as buffalo grazing land quite low. For the whites interested in intensive agriculture or in gold mining, on the other hand, the per-acre value of the land was quite high. These very different values would have a big impact on the distribution of the gains from trade or the spoils of war.

That harms were created when whites intruded on Indian lands cannot be disputed. "When the white and red races met on the American frontier there occurred innumerable violations of the personal and property rights of one group by members of the other" (Prucha, 1962, p. 188). The Europeans, holding titles that traced back to their respective sovereigns under a property rights system that made no provision for Indian ownership, steadily encroached on Indian lands. To Indians, however, the Europeans were intruders who had no rights to the land.

Once whites intruded into Indian territory, two factors determined whether Indians asserted claims to the disputed resources. First, asserting a claim depended on the expected loss from a continuing trespass. If the land in dispute was not very valuable, either to the Indians themselves or to others willing to trade for the land, it might not be worth it for Indians to assert a claim. Second, even if the value of the land was high, it might not be worth asserting a claim if the costs of negotiating a settlement or fighting were high. Neither of these points suggests that the actions of the whites were right. However, there are costs to defending property rights, and these costs, relative to the value of the property in question, will determine whether a claim is asserted and defended.

In the absence of an ideological commitment to respecting the rights to another's claim, asserting and defending a claim requires a credible ability to fight. Even if negotiation is the aim, contracting is more difficult when the other side has the physical ability simply to take.[3] Therefore, only in cases where Indian rights were valuable enough to warrant defense (that is, where Indians had sufficient military power to make a credible threat) would bargaining and exchange result following trespass by whites.

Given that Indians were willing and able to assert a claim against the trespassers, the question for both parties was whether to settle peacefully or fight. The factors in this decision are quite complex and depend extensively on bargaining strategies.[4] Suffice it to say that if the parties could bargain costlessly and if each party knew precisely the military strength of its opponent and the value the opponent placed on the land, few disputes would result in fights. On the other hand, if bargaining were costly due to differences in language, customs, and property institutions and if there was asymmetry in the information about relative fighting strengths, battles would be more likely. Consider how these variables changed over the course of the nineteenth century.

Removal of Intruders

As marked by the first Thanksgiving, early interactions between whites and Indians were not necessarily confrontational. This can be explained by the fact that the land and resources initially desired by the whites was small in comparison to what the Indians had. Moreover, to the Indians, giving up a little land was a small price to pay for the opportunity to trade with the whites who had goods of high value to the Indians. In 1625 New England colonists asked the Pemaquid tribe to give them 12,000 acres of Pemaquid land, which the tribe did in "the first deed of Indian land to English colonists" (Brown, 1970, p. 3). As Utley describes conditions on the Great Plains until about the time of the Mexican War, white intrusions were not worth the Indians' while to stop, although whites' behavior was "sometimes reprehensible. . . . Neither race posed much of a threat to the other, and on the whole they got along fairly well" (1967, p. 59).

Historians generally agree that peaceful negotiations were more prevalent than battles in the history of Indian-white relations. "More than generally appreciated, the contact [between Indians and whites] was even friendly, or at least peaceful" (Utley, 1984, p. xx). Roback summarizes Indian-white relations in colonial times: "Europeans generally acknowledged that the Indians retained possessory rights to their lands. More importantly, the English recognized the advantage of being on friendly terms with the Indians. Trade with the Indians, especially the fur trade, was profitable. War was costly" (1992, p. 11). Even after the French and Indian War, by which the English deemed themselves to have won French rights to land in the New World, "there was no assumption that Indian rights in the lands claimed by France had been extinguished. Although Indian rights were less formal and less fundamental in European eyes than European claims, they nevertheless did exist as the subject for purchase, for negotiation, for retention" (Washburn, 1971, p. 49).

The legal doctrine that guided U.S. policy toward Indians in the late eighteenth and early nineteenth centuries "recognized the Indians' right to use and occupy land. Under this title, the United States is liable to pay the tribe when it decides to extinguish the Indian use and occupancy" (Kickingbird & Ducheneaus, 1973, p. 7). In supporting Indian land rights, Thomas Jefferson asserted that the United States had a "sole and exclusive right to purchasing from them whenever they should be willing to sell" (quoted in Washburn, 1971, p. 56). Even though this preemption theory adhered to by Jefferson gave the United States the sole right to negotiate with the Indians, it did not provide

> any dominion, or jurisdiction, or paramountship
> whatever, but merely in the nature of a remainder
> after the extinguishment of the present right, which
> gave us no present right whatever, but of preventing
> other nations from taking possession, and so defeat-
> ing our expectancy; that the Indians had the full,
> undivided and independent sovereignty as long as
> they chose to keep it, and that this might be forever.
> (Jefferson quoted in Washburn, 1971, p. 39)

Thomas Jefferson found land acquisition by negotiation had
been the norm, and land takings not extensive, noting

> that the lands of this country were taken from them
> [Indians] by conquest, is not so general a truth as is
> supposed. I find in our historians and records, re-
> peated proofs of purchase, which cover a considerable
> part of the lower country; and many more would
> doubtless be found on further search. The upper coun-
> try we know has been acquired altogether by pur-
> chases made in the most unexceptionable form.
> (1787/1955/96)

Felix Cohen, perhaps the most thorough legal scholar of Indian
property rights, referred to this early period as one of "fair
dealing." He estimated that some $800 million had been paid
for Indian lands by 1947 and concluded that paying
"$800,000,000 for a principle is not a common occurrence in the
world's history" (Cohen, 1947, pp. 32, 46).

Where trespass onto Indian lands did occur during the late
eighteenth and early nineteenth centuries, it was initially the
policy of the U.S. government to protect Indian rights and to
expel white intruders.

> Intrusions upon the lands of the friendly Indian tribes
> is not only a violation of the laws, but in direct
> opposition to the policy of the government towards its
> savage neighbors. Upon application of any Indian
> Agent, stating that intrusions of this nature have
> been committed, and are continued, the President
> requires, that they [whites] shall be equally removed,

and their house and improvements destroyed by military force; and that every attempt to return, shall be repressed in the same manner.[5] (Prucha, 1962, p. 139)

During these early years, U.S. troops were respected by the Indians who saw them not as aggressors but as protectors of Indian rights. Prucha disagrees with "the widely held opinion that the Indians were ruthlessly dispossessed with nothing done to protect their rights. On the contrary, the Indians were not completely deserted. Explicit treaties were made guaranteeing their rights, and stringent laws were enacted to ensure respect for the treaties" (1962, p. 143). During the early years, what military troops there were in Indian Country were seen more as a force for protection of Indian rights than as "a wedge for whites to intrude into forbidden lands" (p. 145).

The idea that conflicts between Indians and whites over land from the very first interaction were settled by violence is erroneous. In part, there were fewer conflicts because there were fewer whites on the frontier. Where violence did occur during the early years of interface, it was often due to the inability of the governments of both sides to prevent their principals from violating the terms of agreements. Most treaty violations were committed "not by leaders of the United States or of the Indian tribes but rather by members of these groups who could not be controlled by the leadership" (Roback, 1992, p. 5). Indeed, chiefs almost never constrained individual warriors. The Nez Perce warrior was typical as he

> accorded his loyalty and allegiance first to his family, then to his band, and finally to his tribe, but rarely beyond.... The autonomous bands looked to chiefs and headmen who counseled but did not command.... [Warriors] obeyed or disobeyed as personal inclination dictated, and combat usually took the form of the explosion of personal encounters rather than a collision of organized units. (Utley, 1984, pp. 7–8)

"Chiefs rarely represented their people as fully as white officials assumed, nor could they enforce compliance if the people did not want to comply" (Utley, 1984, p. 44). Individual warriors frequently ignored the treaties that their chiefs had signed, bringing retribution on the whole tribe or band by whites. The bloody Sioux uprising in Minnesota and massacre of Black Kettle's Cheyenne on the Washita are two infamous examples.[6]

On the white side, similar problems of controlling citizens complicated the interaction with Indians. Treaties signed in good faith by white politicians proved to be unenforceable, as individual whites violated them with impunity. For example, removal of the Five Civilized Tribes was deemed desirable as the only way to protect Indians from whites. The problem lay with the national government's inability to defend local property rights against local white citizens. This problem was recognized from an early date by Secretary of War, Henry Knox, who wrote to President Washington that

> The desires of too many frontier white people, to seize, by force or fraud, upon the neighboring Indian lands has been, and still continues to be, an unceasing cause of jealousy and hatred on the part of the Indians. . . . Revenge is sought, and the innocent frontier people are too frequently involved as victims in the cruel contest. This appears to be the principal cause of the Indian wars. (quoted in Prucha, 1962, p. 156)

It appears that the problem of enforcing agreements on both sides was more a function of being unable to control citizens than of not recognizing the costs of warfare.

The Rise of the Military Bureaucracy

There was a significant increase in the incidence of violence to settle disputes especially after the middle of the nineteenth century (see Table 4.1). Although battles between Indians and whites at first were fewer than treaties negotiated, this pattern was reversed as the nineteenth century progressed. Ultimately, warfare became the principal way of resolving controversy. Over time, the value of resources in Indian Country rose for whites and Indians alike, but this only explains why the exchange price would be higher; it does not explain the shift to warfare. This shift can be attributed to the following factors, but the last seems to be especially significant:

- changing military technology,
- information asymmetries,
- property rights and other transaction cost problems, and
- the rise of the standing army following the Civil War.

Changing Military Technology

It is commonly held that white military superiority allowed easy taking of Indian territory during the nineteenth century. To be sure, whites' warfare technology improved with the introduction of breech-loading and repeating rifles, for example. It is not obvious, however, that whites consistently had systematically better technology. In the early years, for example, Indians' bows and arrows were a match for whites' muskets. Walter Prescott Webb (1931) considers battle between early Texans armed with single-shot long rifles and Comanches armed with bow and arrow.

> In most respects the Indian had the best of it. In the first place, the Texan carried at most three shots; the Comanche carried twoscore or more arrows. It took the Texan a minute to reload his weapon; the Indian could in that time ride three hundred yards and discharge twenty arrows. The Texan had to dismount in order to use his rifle effectively at all, and it was his most reliable weapon; the Indian remained mounted throughout the combat. Apparently the one advantage possessed by the white man was a weapon of longer range and more deadly accuracy than the Indian's bow, but the agility of the Indian and the rapidity of his movements did much to offset this advantage. (p. 169)

In later years, whites' technology improved markedly, as fast-loading rifles and revolvers were invented. But this did not give whites any systematic advantage over the long run. Indians usually were able to obtain new weapons (from both private traders and even the Bureau of Indian Affairs' reservation agents) almost as soon as they were available to troops. And, as Custer's troops discovered, white technology was not always superior and certainly was not enough to guarantee success against large numbers. General Sherman stated that "fifty Indians could checkmate three thousand troops" (quoted in Debo, 1970, p. 221). "Frontier army officers often called the horse warriors the finest light cavalry in the world, and historians have repeated the judgment ever since" (Utley, 1967, p. 7).

The importance of changing white technology in the switch from peaceful negotiation to warfare can be tested by examining the ratio of whites to Indians killed in battle over time. Systematic technological improvements by one side or the other would have an ambiguous effect on the absolute number of deaths because better technology for whites would make them more eager to fight, but it would make Indians less eager to do so. Better white technology, however, should decrease the *ratio* of white to Indian deaths in those battles that were fought, but this ratio does not show a statistically significant decline between 1850 and 1891.[7] Thus, measured in terms of the ratio of white to Indian deaths, changing relative military technology does not appear to have been a significant factor in explaining the resort to battles.

Information Asymmetries

While better technology alone may not have been a sufficient condition for increased warfare, differential information about that technology certainly contributed. To understand the importance of informational asymmetries, recognize that neither side in a dispute would have much incentive to fight if both sides were well informed about the ability of the other to defend its claim. With the likely outcomes well known by both sides, there is less incentive to enter into the negative-sum game of war.[8] When one side or the other is misinformed about the probability of victory, however, the odds of fighting relative to negotiating increase.

From the beginning of contact with Indians, whites understood the importance of providing their opponents with accurate information about white military superiority. Whites continually shipped Indians back to Europe to impress them with the extent of white technology and population, returning them "with the expectation that upon their return they would spread the gospel of European superiority throughout their native villages" (Axtell, 1988, p. 140). Well into the nineteenth century this practice continued. After Sitting Bull's Sioux band fled to Canada, he sent a delegation back to the United States to discuss the possibility of returning.

> [The Indians] were deeply interested in various ac-
> tivities south of the border, such as bridge-building
> and long-range rifle practice, but they seemed espe-
> cially impressed by the telegraph and telephone.
> [General Miles] decided to work on this. He had
> blankets draped across the window of the telegraph
> office in order that they might see the spark leap from
> the key to the contact point. This was shrewd, because
> after watching the spark for a while they agreed
> among themselves that it exceeded the best medicine
> of the Sioux.
>
> Miles then demonstrated the frightful power of
> the telephone. Half of the visitors were escorted to a
> house some distance away, a phone was cranked up,
> and they were instructed to talk to each other. When
> they recognized the voices of distant friends speaking
> the Dakota language, he says, "huge drops of perspi-
> ration coursed down their bronze faces and with trem-
> bling hand they laid the instrument down." These
> were men who had endured the torture of the Sun
> Dance and had been ready to give their lives at the
> Little Bighorn, but after this horrifying experience
> they became urgent advocates of peace. (Connell,
> 1988, p. 218)

As the frontier moved west, however, information asymmetries increased for several reasons. Since western Indians
were more nomadic, it was more difficult for whites to communicate with an entire tribe. To be sure, nomadic Plains Indians
regularly were taken to Washington to be impressed by the
power of the federal government and the growing white population. But the information did not always filter down to wan-
dering bands, or it simply was not believed.

On the white side, the different landscape and climate on
the Plains resulted in Indian warfare tactics different from
what whites had encountered previously. And Indians' nomadic

existence meant that whites often had poor information about the number of hostiles opposing them. The Plains Indians "greatly favored the decoy tactic" (Utley, 1984, p. 105), sending forth a small party to encounter a white detachment, seemingly by mistake, and then running from it to lure pursuing whites into a trap where far more numerous Indian warriors lay hidden.

In fact, one side's faulty information seems to have been an important factor in just about all the bloody fighting in the West. In the notorious 1866 Fetterman Massacre, 81 bluecoats were enticed into combat with some 2000 Sioux by the decoy tactic and were wiped out. Custer's apparent foolhardiness in attacking over three thousand Sioux and Cheyenne with just a few hundred men at the Little Bighorn in 1876 simply reflects his ignorance of the true number of Indians opposing him.[9]

The Wagon Box Fight in 1867, in which the Sioux suffered extraordinarily heavy losses, illustrates how changing military technology contributed to the informational asymmetry. "One chief placed them [Sioux losses] at 1,137, and called the battle a 'medicine fight'—meaning that the soldiers had supernatural help. What the soldiers had were new Springfield breech-loading rifles and plenty of ammunition, while the Indians were using the old muzzle-loaders" (Chapel, 1961, p. 259). When the revolver was first used by the Texas Rangers in the 1840s, the Indians were shocked by its effect. After being attacked by a numerically superior band of Comanches in Nueces Canyon, the Texas Rangers pursued the Indians on horseback firing their pistols. "Never was a band of Indians more surprised than at this charge," said one of the Rangers (quoted in Webb, 1931, p. 174). After a chase that covered 300 miles and resulted in more than 100 Indian deaths, "a Comanche chief who was in this fight said he never wanted to fight Jack Hays and his Rangers again" because "they had a shot for every finger on the hand" (Webb, 1931, p. 175). Hence, it was not just new military technology but the element of surprise in the introduction of that technology that contributed to fighting instead of negotiating. Once it was clear that one side had superior military technology, however, like the Comanche chief, the Indians would have little taste for another fight.

Property Rights and Other Transaction Cost Problems

If ownership rights to property are well defined and can be exchanged, the costs of negotiations decline relative to the costs of taking. If whites knew which tribe "owned" a parcel of land and knew with whom to bargain, the costs of negotiated settlements were lower and the likelihood of settlements higher. Conversely, if Indians did not have clear, transferable property rights, whites desiring the land had little alternative but to take.

In this regard there were important differences between Indian tribes east and west of the Mississippi. As noted in Chapter 2, in the East, where agriculture was the principal commercial activity, private property was more common. Under such sedentary conditions, ownership claims to parcels of land were clear, and Indian political institutions made negotiations easier.

Indian institutions west of the Mississippi were different, however, because of the horse. Prior to the horse, many of the great nomadic hunting and warrior tribes of the West practiced sedentary agriculture with ownership institutions similar to the Creek. The horse and the gun dislodged Indians from centuries-old ancestral lands and institutions by making it more productive for Indians to rove in pursuit of the buffalo. This new way of life on the Plains created conflict among Indians even before the whites arrived on the scene. As one Sioux chief declared to his white conquerors, "You have split my land and I don't like it. These lands once belonged to the Kiowas and the Crows, but we whipped these nations out of them, and in this we did what the white men do when they want the lands of the Indians" (quoted in Utley, 1984, p. 61). White migration did not intrude on an equilibrium system of aboriginal rights respected by Indians themselves "but rather broke over a congeries of scattered groups that had been fighting one another for generations and would continue to fight one another to the day of final conquest by the whites" (Utley, 1984, p. 11).

For the nomadic tribes, land and the resources on it were held communally with only usufruct rights by possession recognized.

> All the natives . . . venerated their homeland and looked upon it with a keen sense of possession. It was

a group possession, however, recognizing the right of all to partake of its bounty. No individual could "own" any part of it to the exclusion of others. Use privileges might be granted or sold, but sale of the land itself was a concept foreign to the Indian mind. (Utley, 1984, pp. 8–9)

Without clearly defined property rights that could be bought and sold, it is not surprising that armed conflict replaced negotiation.

The Rise of the Standing Army

Perhaps the most important factor contributing to increased fighting between whites and Indians was the rise of the standing U.S. Army. In the first years of the new republic, the militia system was common: "Individual colonies, and more often the frontiersmen themselves, had to protect the frontier" (Beers, 1975, p. 173). But especially after the War of 1812, the federal government had the army build and garrison a growing line of forts. "The defense of the Indian frontier was a contribution of the government of the United States to its [white] citizens" (p. 173).

Maintaining a standing army, as opposed to raising a militia, predictably would increase the number of battles. Once the fixed costs of raising troops was incurred, the additional cost of fighting was lower and hence the likelihood of fighting higher. A standing army meant full-time officers and, behind them, military bureaucrats, whose careers and budgets were advanced by fighting wars.

It was in this way that the buildup of a large standing army contributed to the demise of Indian-white negotiations. Following both the Mexican and Civil Wars, the size of the peacetime army had to shrink. This was acceptable to most enlisted men, who were volunteers. But reduced troop strength was of considerable concern to career officers. There were simply not enough positions to go around, as a mission of high-ranking army officers under Major General William Tecumseh Sherman found while visiting the West in 1866:

The Civil War had ended, and the dissolution of the great volunteer armies had been all but completed.

Yet the exact form and dimensions of the peacetime army had not been fixed, and the high command was encumbered by an embarrassing surplus of colonels and generals for whom positions remained to be found. (Utley, 1967, p. xi)

While many enlisted men might have been happy to return home to civilian duties, the career officers had little opportunity for promotion. "A man might win brevets galore for bravery and skill in the red smoke of battle and still find himself at his old grade when the smoke blew away—a dismal man rotting in the dull round of the years, waiting like a ghoul for some other officer up ahead of him on the register to die in bed" (Lewis, 1950, p. 321).

For these officers, the "Indian problem" provided an excellent way to ensure that the "red smoke of battle" did not blow away. "Protection of the frontier population and travel routes from hostile Indians placed the largest demand on the Army. . . . For [the latter half of the nineteenth century], the U.S. Army would find its primary mission and its main reason for existence in the requirements of the westward movement beyond the Mississippi" (Utley, 1967, pp. 2–3). The individuals involved understood the benefits of fighting. Civil War officers retained their brevet ranks and pay as long as they were fighting Indians. For enlisted men as well as officers, an absence of war meant ennui and lost chances for advancement.

It was dismal, frustrating duty. Boredom, low pay, coarse food and shabby quarters, harsh discipline and cruel punishment, constant labor of an unmilitary character, field service marked by heat and cold, rain and snow, mud and dust, hunger and thirst, deadening fatigue—these were to be expected. But they were unaccompanied by the prospect of meaningful combat and the opportunity for distinction that ordinarily make the terms of military life more endurable. (Utley, 1967, pp. 110–111)

The antidote was battle, but the excuse for battle was not necessarily easy to come by. After inspecting the Smoky Hill stage line through the Cheyenne and Arapaho hunting grounds, General Sherman remarked, "God only knows when, and I do not see how, we can make a decent excuse for an Indian war" (Debo, 1970, p. 215). But he also "made cynical reference to the local hunger for army contracts. Usually citizens were happy to call on the regular army to do the shooting, especially as federal troops required supplies bought locally. This factor often caused citizens to holler loudly before they were hurt" (Russell, 1973, p. 47). Politicians also were quick to recognize that fighting meant increased federal revenues in their districts.[10] In short, the Indian Wars found part of their roots in a strong coalition of professional soldiers, politicians, suppliers, and citizens.

The anecdotal evidence that the rise of a standing army increased the number of battles with Indians is supported by empirical data. During the nineteenth century, the army grew principally through two wars. In 1845, the U.S. Army totaled 8509 officers and enlisted men. With the onset of the Mexican War (1846–1848), however, the Army grew almost sixfold to 47,319 and never returned to pre-war size. In 1860 the Army numbered over 16,000. But during the Civil War (1861–1865), the Union Army grew to a phenomenal 1 million men by 1865. It never shrank to pre-war levels, fluctuating between 25,000 and 30,000 men in the 1870s and 1880s. Even during the Civil War the number of troops in the West increased. "Between 1861 and 1865 two million men sprang to the defense of the union. . . . Many of these men discovered that they had volunteered for duty against enemies clad in breechclout and feathers rather than Confederate gray. By 1865 almost twenty thousand soldiers, mostly volunteers, served in the West, about double the 1860 figure" (Utley, 1984, p. 70).

If having a standing army increases the propensity to fight rather than negotiate, the number of Indian battles should rise after both the Mexican War and the Civil War. Table 4.2 confirms this hypothesis, showing that the mean number of battles in the five years following the two wars was significantly higher than in the five years preceding each war.[11] A regression analysis makes possible the estimation of the impact of the standing army on the increasing tendency for battles.[12] The data show that the Mexican War caused a discontinuous increase of almost 11 battles per year, and the Civil War caused

TABLE 4.2   Indian Battles Before and After the Mexican and Civil Wars

Years	Mean annual number of battles
1841–1845	2.8
1849–1854	8.4

Means significantly different at .01 level (t = 2.61).

1856–1860	31.6
1865–1869	110.4

Means significantly different at .01 level (t = 4.09).

an increase of approximately 25 battles per year. There is no escaping the fact that a standing army reduced the incentive for whites to negotiate with Indians.

Conclusion

The changing benefits and costs of negotiating to resolve disputes between Indians and whites during the nineteenth century helps explain the evolution toward warfare. The whites arrived in the New World expecting to find the riches of India but instead found a vast tract of land uninhabited by European standards. Once it became clear that this land contained resources of value in the Old World, Europeans faced two choices; they could trade or raid. Which they chose depended on the terms of trade, including all the costs of negotiating relative to the costs of fighting. Initially, both Indians and whites chose trading over fighting. For Indians well-endowed with land, the value of trade goods offered by the Europeans far exceeded the value of the natural endowment. Moreover, at the time of initial contact, the whites were outnumbered and possessed a military technology ill-suited for using force against the Indians. Hence, treaties dominated Indian-white relations for the first half of the nineteenth century.

A growing white population increased the demand for

Indian land, but this only meant that whites were willing to pay more. They could have paid in the form of higher offers but chose instead to pay in the form of higher military expenditures. This shift away from trading toward raiding was closely tied to the rise of the standing army following the Mexican and Civil wars. Throughout the nineteenth century, the U.S. government paid millions of dollars for Indian lands, but on average it paid only 50 percent of fair market value.[13] Part of the reason the federal government was able to obtain Indian land for less than fair market value was its ability to threaten force. Statistical evidence for the nineteenth century shows that bringing an additional 100 troops into an area where whites wanted land decreased the actual price paid for the land relative to its fair market value by 2 percentage points.[14]

The Indian wars following the Civil War show the important role of politics in collective decisions to raid or trade. Particularly with the substitution of a standing army for local militias, war rather than negotiation became a tool for politically potent groups in the United States. Certainly the adage that "might makes right" is not morally acceptable, but Indian policy in the last half of the nineteenth century shows that "might makes rights" was politically acceptable. As raiding replaced trading for Indian resources, the late nineteenth and early twentieth centuries saw the fate of American Indians move away from their homelands and into the political arena in Washington.

Notes

1. This chapter is partly extracted from Anderson and McChesney (1994).

2. The logic of this discussion follows the economics of dispute resolution. Parties to disputes can either settle out of court or litigate to the bitter end. For a summary of how this approach has been used in the economics literature, see Cooter and Rubinfield (1989).

3. This point is similar to Umbeck's conclusion that "rights to property can exist only as long as other people agree to respect them or as long as the owner can forcefully exclude those who do not agree" (1981, p. 45).

4. For a more rigorous discussion, see Anderson and McChesney (1994).

5. See Secretary of War William H. Crawford's Memo to Military Commanders, January 27, 1816, quoted in Prucha (1962).

6. The 1862 Sioux uprising began when a group of Indian youths murdered five whites. "The deed had not been planned. One had dared another to prove his courage" (Utley, 1984, p. 78). The Washita massacre occurred because Black Kettle, a Cheyenne chief who persistently argued for peace with whites, "had a hard time keeping his young men under control" (Utley, 1984, p. 125). When a group of braves slipped away to raid white settlements, their trail in the snow led back to Black Kettle's village. Cavalry under General Custer followed the trail, stormed the village, and killed over 100 Cheyenne, including Black Kettle.

7. For the formal statistics, see Anderson and McChesney (1994). Even when the outlier for Custer's Last Stand is removed, the difference is not significant. A regression was also run to determine whether there was any upward trend over time in the ratio, and none was found.

8. For a more theoretical discussion of this point, see the model presented by Anderson and McChesney (1994).

9. For a discussion of Custer's faulty information regarding Indian strength, see Connell (1988, pp. 263–264).

10. For further discussion, see Utley (1967, pp. 14–17).

11. The test might seem subject to the criticism that while the army was away fighting, Indians took advantage of this absence to increase attacks on whites, with the army ultimately returning

to subdue the tribes. However, as already noted, the number of troops in the West actually increased during the Civil War.

12. For a full discussion of this regression analysis, see Anderson and McChesney (1994).

13. For a discussion of how much was paid for Indian lands relative to "fair market value," see Wishart (1990). In five of the 40 cases studied by Wishart, Indians received no initial compensation for their land, but in 16 of the cases they received fair market value. This suggests that even though the average compensation was low relative to fair market values, Indians did not always end up with the short end of the bargain.

14. For a full discussion of the tradeoffs between paying for Indian land and investing in military troops, see Wood (1992).

CHAPTER 5

Bureaucracy versus Indians

The rise of the standing army dramatically changed the interface between Indians and whites, but it was only the tip of the bureaucratic iceberg that came to dominate the lives of Indians. From an early date, Congress and the Supreme Court contended that tribes were to be treated as sovereigns, but Indians became wards of the state with politicians and bureaucrats in Washington, D.C., acting as their trustees. Not surprisingly, the effect has not always been maximization of Indian welfare. But it has surely meant the growth of the bureaucracy, as can be seen in Table 5.1. Taylor concludes from these data that "the implementation of federal Indian policy has required personnel and organization, and from a very small beginning the organization has become one of the largest civilian bureaus in the government" (1984, p. 35).

When the whites did succeed in conquering the Plains Indians, discontinuous institutional change was forced on the red man by the federal government. During a brief time of self-determination on the reservations, Indians again demonstrated their adaptability in response to necessity. Because agriculture was necessary for survival, they developed an institutional structure under which crop and livestock production increased. Even during the early years of allotment when the government was assigning parcels of land to individual Indians, "relative security of legal title created an opportunity for enterprising individuals to regain a limited degree of independence from the ration list. Farming and ranching also gave ambitious men an opportunity to accumulate wealth outside the Bureau of Indian Affairs' patronage system and, through sharing and gifting, to establish themselves as autonomous leaders" (Barsh, 1987, p. 85).

However, when the government imposed new institutions on the Indians, agricultural productivity suffered because politicization of the institutions exhibited a blatant disregard for existing and past cultural norms. Barsh (1987) describes the traditional Plains Indian government

> as an open-ended meritocracy with many gently competing poles of authority. Individual freedom was ensured by the representation of all families in council and by the requirement of consensus for national action. Equally important was the nature of the economy, which rewarded coordination but did not make it necessary for survival. Even the smallest family, functioning as a cooperative economic unit, could provide for itself under most circumstances. Only in times of war or disaster were wider economic and security arrangements unavoidable. Government

TABLE 5.1 Total Number of Employees in Bureau of Indian Affairs by Year

Year	Number of Employees
1852	108
1888	1,725
1911	6,000
1933	5,000
1934	12,000
since 1934	11,000 to 16,000

Source: Taylor (1959, p. 98).

therefore functioned "at need" rather than as a permanent, coercive establishment. (p. 84)

But after relegation to reservations, government became both permanent and coercive. "When we hear it said today that Indians do not believe in property or in private enterprise, we are still hearing the echoes of the struggle against Indian agrarian entrepreneurs in the 1930s—a struggle waged in the name of liberating landless Indians from poverty, but which in reality returned reservation economies to government dependence" (Barsh, 1987, p. 89).

Rather than fighting the army on the frontier, Indians found that the battles over reservations shifted to Washington, D.C. The 1887 General Allotment Act was one of the first laws to specify how reservation land would be allocated. Under this act, reservation land was to be allotted to individual Indians in much the same way that the federal domain was to be transferred to private individuals under the Homestead Act. Backers of the Dawes Act touted it as a necessary ingredient for improving the welfare of Indians. As Senator Dawes himself put it, "Till this people will consent to give up their lands, and divide them among their citizens so that each can own the land he cultivates, they will not make much progress" (cited in Otis, 1973, pp. 10–11). Carlson notes that "no student of property-rights literature or, indeed, economic theory will be surprised that the complicated and heavily supervised property right that emerged from allotment led to inefficiencies, corruption, and losses for both Indians and society" (1981, p. 174). One of the major costs of transferring land to non-Indians may have been the reduced sense of an ethnic community on reservations. McChesney (1992) calls this an "ethnic externality," meaning that outside customs and cultures made it harder to maintain tribal customs and culture.

Juxtaposed against the arguments that the Dawes Act was pushed by social do gooders to improve Indian welfare and assimilate them into the white man's culture is the special interest theory of politics. Under this theory, laws are passed because they confer benefits upon interest groups that are influential in the political arena. In this case, the General Allotment Act formed the proverbial "iron triangle" of politics in which white settlers got the land, politicians received votes, and bureaucrats increased their budgets. In this chapter, I will develop the special interest theory of government as it applies to Indian policy.

Public versus Private Interest

The guardianship model of Indian policy explains the relationship between the federal government and Indians as an effort by the government to correct imperfections in the institutional structure on Indian reservations. Many reformers saw allotment as the only way to "Americanize" the Indian. The "friends of the Indian," including missionaries, clergymen, bureaucrats, educators, and journalists, met annually in Lake Mohonk, New York, for the purpose of making Indians equal citizens in the young republic. According to Prucha (1973), the reformers built their policy on three proposals:

> first, to break up the tribal relations and their reservation base and to individualize the Indian on a 160 acre homestead . . . ; second, to make the Indians citizens and equal with the whites in regard to both the protection and restraints of law; and third, to provide a universal government school system that would make good Americans out of the rising generation of Indians. (p. 6)

If Indians were to be Americanized, reformers thought they would have to abandon their communal way of life. "What the allotment debaters meant by communism was that title to the land was dependent on its use and occupancy. They meant vaguely the cooperatives and clannishness—the strong communal sense—of barbaric life" (Otis, 1973, pp. 11–12). Overcoming this communism meant adopting a system of private property rights on reservations similar to that evolving under the Homestead Act. Carlson concludes that "reformers came to see allotment as the panacea for the problems of American Indians" (1981, p. 8), thus making "it difficult to find statements opposing the proposal" (Prucha, 1973, p. 122).

On February 8, 1887, the General Allotment Act was passed, giving the president of the United States authority to assign parcels of land on reservations to individual Indians. In his 1887 Annual Report, the Commissioner of Indian Affairs asserted that this act would "finally enable the Government to leave the Indian to stand alone" (1887, p. viii).

While a few tribes were exempted from the legislation, most found themselves with the head of household being assigned 160 acres, although the allotment size varied widely across reservations from as little as 10 acres to as much as 400 acres. Large allotments tended to be located in arid regions, and the smallest allotments tended to result when the original reservation acreage was insufficient to be divided into 160-acre parcels for all Indian families. An adult Indian was given four years to choose his parcels, and if he failed or refused to do so within that time, the Secretary of the Interior was to assign an allotment to him. After all eligible members of the tribe received their allotments, the General Allotment Act stated that all remaining lands were surplus and opened to "secure homes for actual settlers."[1] Prior to 1900 these surplus lands were purchased from the tribe by the federal government and settlers were allowed to homestead. After the turn of the century, the government sold the lands to whites on behalf of the tribes.

The dates when reservations were allotted varied considerably across Indian Country. On some reservations, allotment ensued the first year after the Dawes Act, whereas on others allotment did not take place until after 1930. Some reservations, most notably those in the Southwest, were not allotted at all, thereby maintaining tribal ownership of most reservation land.

Once allotted, the lands originally were to be held in trust by the federal government for 25 years, at the end of which time the Indian was to receive full fee simple title to the land. During the period of trusteeship, the land was not to be sold, leased, or willed to another Indian or non-Indian. But because many allotted lands were not coming into production, the act was amended in 1891 to permit leasing with the result that "leasing soon became more prevalent than working one's own plot on many reservations" (McChesney, 1992, p. 114). In fact Prucha reports that 112,000 acres out of 140,000 acres of allotted lands on the Omaha and Winnebago reservations were leased by 1898 (1984, p. 673). The 1906 amendment to the General Allotment

Act authorized the Secretary of Interior to issue fee patents immediately if any Indian was deemed "competent and capable of managing his or her affairs."

> These changes, particularly the general availability of fee patents, marked a "radical switch" from the more paternalistic role established for the federal government by the Dawes Act. From 1913 to 1920 issuance of fee patents became the top priority of the Indian Office. Between 1917 and 1920, there were 10,956 fee patents issued, compared with 9,894 issued between 1906 and 1916. (McChesney, 1992, p. 114)

When fee simple title to allotted lands or surplus lands passed to individuals, the land was no longer considered "Indian Land"—even if it was owned by an Indian. Hence, the total amount of Indian land declined dramatically between 1871 and 1983 (see Table 5.2) as fee simple patents were issued by the federal government. Measured in terms of privatization, the General Allotment Act was incredibly effective; measured in terms of Indian ownership, however, it was a disaster. According to Washburn, "about 60 percent of this land passed out of Indian hands" (1971, p. 145).

Given that so many acres were transferred from Indian to white hands under this act, a special interest theory of politics provides an alternative to the "guardianship model" (see Carlson, 1981, p. 33) of allotment. According to this theory, non-Indian special interest groups would seek legislation that would enable these groups to capture the wealth of reservations through political processes. With reservations being established at precisely the time when western land values were rising, whites who were excluded from settling these reservations had an incentive to find a mechanism to obtain access. The General Allotment Act provided this access by allowing them to purchase land from allottees or tribes or to homestead the surplus. As a result, non-Indians ended up on the receiving end of "one of the largest real estate transfers in history" (Carlson, 1981, p. 18).

If the white settlers were the demanders of this legislation, the politicians and bureaucrats were the suppliers. As Alston and Spiller note, demand side theories of regulation "neglect the supply side of legislation—the institutions that enact legislation" (1992, p. 86). Senators and congressmen on influential congressional committees

> self-select across committees according to the nature of their constituents; those with particular interest in the allocation of Indian lands, for example, would self-select to the committees on Indian affairs. Within a committee those with more seniority also command

TABLE 5.2   Indian Lands (Acres), 1871–1983

Year	Tribal Lands	Allotted	Total
1871	111,761,558	10,231,725	121,993,283
1881	139,006,794	14,625,518	155,632,312
1887	119,375,930	17,018,965	136,394,895
1890	86,540,824	17,773,525	104,314,349
1890	86,540,824	17,773,525	140,314,349
1900	52,455,827	25,409,546	77,865,373
1911[a]	40,263,442	32,272,420	72,535,862
1920	35,501,661	37,158 655	72,660,316
1929	32,014,945	39,129,268	71,144,213
1933	29,481,685	40,106,736	69,588,421
1939[b]	35,402,440	17,594,376	52,996,816
1945	37,288,768	17,357,540	54,646,308
1953	42,785,935	14,674,763	57,460,698
1962	38,814,074	11,763,160	50,557,234
1974	40,772,934	10,244,481	51,017,415
1979	41,803,230	10,058,445	51,861,675
1983	42,385,031	10,226,180	52,611,211

Notes: [a] After 1911, allotted land includes allotments that were alienated and thus not in trust status. [b] The allotted acreages after 1933 include only allotted lands that remained in individual trust status. For example, the data indicate that, as of 1933, more than 40 million acres had been allotted, of which 25,277,322 acres had been transferred to fee simple status.

Source: Stuart (1987, pp. 15, 18).

more power. Policy, therefore, is skewed toward the preferences of the senior members. Policy may change for one of two reasons: (1) committee membership remains the same and constituents' interests change or (2) committee membership changes and new members have different preferences than those members they replaced. (Alston & Spiller, 1992, p. 86)

Given that Indians constituted a small portion of the population and that many Indians could not or did not vote anyway, congressional committees represented the interests of non-Indian constituents, and policy reflected this. If whites wanted access to Indian lands, they would expect their representatives to deliver the policies that would allow this. The General Allotment Act did this.

In between the voters and the politicians were the bureaucratic middlemen who possess characteristics of both demanders and suppliers. On the demand side, they have an interest in expanding their budgets and other powers, but on the supply side they must provide services for the constituent public on behalf of politicians. In the case of nineteenth-century Indian policy, the Office of Indian Affairs was the dominant and growing bureaucratic player. It supported assimilation of Indians into white America including giving individual Indians rather than the tribes autonomy and privatizing reservation lands.

In principal, it served the individual Indian, but Indians as individuals were permitted little opportunity to influence its policies. Indeed, unallotted Indians could not even vote before 1924. In this situation, the Office of Indian Affairs was not "captured" by Indian tribes and its policies did not systematically reflect the wishes of Indians. The Office of Indian Affairs, however, could be "captured" by other groups that gained or lost as a result of its policies. Ideally, any group that was pro-assimilationist and anti-tribe might be able to align its interests with those of the Office. (Carlson, 1981, p. 36)

In much the same way bootleggers and Baptists aligned with

one another in an unholy alliance to support abolition of liquor sales on the Sabbath,[2] assimilationists and land-hungry settlers supported bureaucratic efforts to allot Indian lands. Under this scenario, the pressure for opening reservations to whites increased as land values rose with settlement pressure.[3]

If land-hungry settlers were the main beneficiaries of allotment policy, why weren't Indians granted outright title to the allotments so that white intrusion could occur faster? Or why wasn't all reservation land declared surplus and opened to homesteading? The answer centers around the desire of the bureaucracy to increase its budget. Had the lands been given directly to Indians or whites, what role would there have been for the Office of Indian Affairs? To be sure, they would have continued to supply Indians with agricultural technology and advice, but allotment allowed the office "to supervise his or her property individually. One sign of these increased administrative costs was the rapid growth of the number of clerks needed in Washington. From 1900 to 1920, the number of employees in the Office of Indian Affairs in Washington increased from 101 to 262" (Carlson, 1981, p. 44). By amending the Dawes Act in 1891 to allow for leasing allotments that had not been released from trusteeship, Congress allowed whites access to the lands while preserving an important role for the bureaucracy. In fact, this gave Indian agents even more power, because it was up to them to determine and enforce the terms of leases. "Leases came to be granted more and more freely, and by the turn of the century, the leasing of allotments was relatively common" (Carlson, 1981, p. 37).

From this special interest theory of allotment three hypotheses follow:

▶ Congressional committee decisions will reflect the demands of constituents, and policies will change as these demands change.

▶ Allotment would occur first in those areas where whites placed a higher value on the land held by Indians.

▶ As the allotment process transferred millions of acres out of BIA control, the bureaucracy would have lost nearly all of its power had it not halted the process by retaining trust authority under the 1934 Indian Reorganization Act.

Consider the evidence supporting these hypotheses.

A Congressional Theory of Indian Property Rights[4]

When conflicts began to occur on the Appalachian frontier in the early 1800s, the basic approach to the problem was "removal of Indians to Indian country based on the belief that there was room and sufficient resources for all and that in the separation of Indians from non-Indians there would be little conflict and no need to be concerned over the Indians' problems" (Taylor, 1984, p. 10). With the passage of the Indian Removal Act in 1830, most of the eastern tribes "moved as a result of persuasion, bribery, or threats" (p. 12). Included in this removal were the Cherokee, who signed a treaty in 1835 ceding their land east of the Mississippi River to the federal government in return for $5 million and 7 million acres west of the Mississippi.

As part of the removal process, the Cherokee eventually were granted title to 6 million acres in northwestern Oklahoma that was to be an "outlet" to their hunting grounds and became known as the Cherokee Outlet. Whatever the value of these lands to the Cherokee as an outlet to hunting grounds, the whites saw its potential for grazing. "Naturally, the Cherokees attempted to reap the return from their claim to the land. Their peculiar legal position as wards of the U.S. government, however, limited the actions they could take. Given the uncertainty of the Cherokees' claim, cattlemen and prospective homesteaders also tried to secure rights to the land" (Alston & Spiller, 1992, p. 85). A battle for the property rights ensued with congressional committees being the arbiter of the disputed claims.

Throughout the history of government policy regarding Indian property rights, those rights often have been ambiguous, leaving the assignment of those rights to bureaucratic discretion. With Indian property rights not clearly specified, Congress and its agencies—such as the Bureau of Indian Affairs—have been in a position to redistribute the sticks in the bundle of rights to special interest constituencies. "In the case of the Cherokee Outlet, legislation did not specify the land use rights of the Cherokees. Because of a lack of specificity, the Cherokee's use of the land was subject to bureaucratic, congressional, and judicial interpretation" (Alston & Spiller, 1992, p. 88).

This ambiguity had its drawbacks to the Cherokees and to the cattlemen who wished to lease the Outlet from the Cherokees, but it did afford Congress the ability to adapt to the changing value of Indian lands. Had Congress simply assigned property rights to the Cherokees, white constituents would have had to deal directly with the Indians, cutting out politicians; had Congress assigned the land to the whites, it would have cut out the Bureau of Indian Affairs. As a balance between these two extremes, Congress chose to leave Indian land policy in the hands of the BIA subject to oversight and funding jurisdiction of House and Senate committees on Indian affairs. Under this oversight system, governmental policy could adapt to changing demands for the Outlet. Over time, policy shifted from allowing the Cherokees to tax cattlemen to blocking the Cherokees from long-term leasing of the land and, ultimately, forcing the Cherokees to sell the Outlet. These changes "transpired without Congress making a definite decision on the matter. Congress, however, was not on the sidelines, nor was the Bureau of Indian Affairs a runaway bureaucracy. Instead, when land prices increased substantially in neighboring areas, Congress undertook an investigation of the leasing practices of the Cherokees. . . . All that it [policy change] took was an action in the appropriations committees" (Alston & Spiller, 1992, pp. 88–89).

In the battle for property rights to the Outlet, the Cherokees were the ultimate losers. Initially, cattlemen driving their animals north to railheads along the Dodge City Trail saw the value of grass in the Outlet and were willing to pay a tax for trespass and grazing. The committees on Indian affairs could have used their power to minimize the burden on cattlemen by disallowing the grazing tax or by not enforcing collection of the tax. They chose, however, in the 1880s to authorize the grazing tax and to allow the use of the U.S. Cavalry to assist in enforcement.[5]

Support for the grazing tax system can be explained by the fact that tax-paying cattlemen saw more security with the taxing arrangement. Some cattlemen even fenced their ranges in the Outlet because it allowed them to exclude the non-taxpayers and the so-called Boomers, farmers advocating white settlement in Indian territory. To improve their bargaining position with the Indians and to more effectively lobby their representatives in Washington, the cattlemen formed the Cherokee Strip Livestock Association (CSLA). The CSLA leased the Outlet from the Indians in 1883 for an annual fee of $100,000, which "pleased the Cherokee Nation and the CSLA" (Alston & Spiller, 1992, p. 90).

But the Boomers continued to flow into the Outlet, prompting both the cattlemen and the Indians to complain to Washington. Although the federal government approved the use of troops to remove the squatters in 1884, "Boomer resistance nudged public opinion and the sympathies of many Congressmen toward the view of the homeseekers" (Alston & Spiller, 1992, p. 91).

The Boomers, CSLA, and Cherokees all realized that land values in the region were rising in response to population growth. When the lease expired in 1888, the CSLA upped their ante for the lease to $175,000, the Indians held out for more and eventually settled for $200,000, and the Boomers continued to pressure Congress to purchase the Outlet and open it for settlement. Ultimately the Boomers won the battle as Congress passed an appropriation bill in 1889 authorizing payment of $1.25 per acre to the Cherokees, and in October 1889 the secretary of the interior ordered the CSLA to remove its cattle from the Outlet. Though the CSLA offered $30 million for the outright purchase of the Outlet, the Cherokees refused the bid, only to be forced later to "'agree' to the sale of the Outlet to the U.S. government for $8.6 million on December 19, 1891" (Alston & Spiller, 1992, p. 92).

The explanation for the Boomer victory is found in the relationship between constituents and their congressional representatives. Though the ranchers were well organized, the Boomers were growing in numbers and by 1870 outnumbered cattlemen in every state bordering the Outlet. The combination of larger numbers and higher land prices provided the necessary demand stimulus for changing the property rights to the Outlet.

The supply side of the story emanates from the Senate committees on Indian Affairs and Appropriations, which dominated Indian policy in the late 1800s. Data on committee membership presented in Table 5.3 and Table 5.4 show that senators from the states bordering and neighboring the Outlet self-selected to the committees important to their constituents. Until 1888, senators from neighboring or bordering states constituted a minimum of four-ninths of the membership on the Senate Committee on Indian Affairs. In 1885 the committee approved a bill passed by the Congress authorizing purchase of the Outlet, but determination of the price was left to the Senate Appropriations Committee. With a majority of that committee representing neighboring or bordering states, it is not surprising that funding for purchase of the Outlet was approved.[6]

Alston and Spiller (1992) draw two policy lessons from the story of the Cherokee Outlet:

> First, because Indians are seldom a recognized special-interest group, their property rights will be continually subject to change unless they are not subject to reallocation through legislation; that is, property rights must be private and not political. Secondly, the

TABLE 5.3   Members of U.S. Senate Committee on Indian Affairs

1876	1880	1884	1886	1888
Allison (IA)*	Coke (TX)*	Dawes (MA)	Dawes (MA)	Dawes (MA)
Oglesby (IL)*	Pendleton (OH)*	Ingalls (KS)*	Ingalls (KS)*	Bowen (CO)
Morrill (ME)	Walker (AK)*	Harrison (IN)*	Harrison (IN)*	Sabin (MN)*
Ingalls (KS)*	Slater (OR)*	Cameron (WI)	Bowen (CO)	Platt (CT)
Clayton (AK)*	Williams (KY)	Bowen (CO)	Sabin (MN)	Stockbridge (MI)
Bogy (MO)*	Allison (IA)*	Coke (TX)*	Maxey (TX)*	Morgan (AL)
McCreery (KY)*	Ingalls (KS)*	Walker (AK)*	Morgan (AL)	Jones (AK)*
	Saunders (NE)	Slater (OR)	Hampton (SC)	Hearst (CA)
	Logan (IL)*	Gorman (MD)	Jones (AK)*	Daniel (VA)

Note: (*) Represents bordering or neighboring state.

Source: Alston and Spiller (1992, p. 100).

TABLE 5.4 Members of Senate Appropriations Committee

_1888_

Allison (IA)*

Dawes (MA)

Plumb (KS)*

Hale (ME)

Farwell (IL)*

Beck (KY)*

Cockrell (MO)*

Call (FL)

Gorman (MD)

Note: (*) Represents states bordering or neighboring the Outlet.

Source: Alston and Spiller (1992, p. 100).

enforcement of property rights is itself a form of government policy that acts through bureaucratic agencies with committee oversight. . . . Thus, the current attention paid by Indians to the actions of the Bureau of Indian Affairs may simply reflect their recognition of the impact of the bureau's enforcement of Indian property rights on the value of Indian resources. (pp. 103–104)

The Demand for Allotment[7]

Just as the Boomers brought pressure to open the Cherokee Outlet for settlement, white farmers saw opportunity on Indian lands all over the West. Throughout the nineteenth century, government land policy had made the public domain available at low prices to those willing to endure the hardships of frontier life. With the Homestead Act beginning in the 1860s, people could obtain title to land by paying a small fee, generally $1.25 per acre, residing on the land for five years, and making improvements on the land. With rising land values in the West as shown in Table 5.5, settlers had an interest in obtaining access to reservation lands.

The passage of the Dawes Act in 1887 provided the whites

access to many, though not all, reservations. Whether and when allotment began varied across reservations, but once the process began, non-Indians had access to Indian land. Lands released from trusteeship could be bought and sold with clear title, and even prior to release they could be leased as a result of congressional action in 1891. Moreover, if there were surplus lands after allotment, those were usually opened to homesteading by anyone.

The demand theory of allotment helps explain when allotment occurred. "The more desirable a reservation was to outsiders, the more pressure they would have placed on the Office of Indian Affairs and the more likely that it would have been allotted sooner" (Carlson, 1981, p. 43). Since survey and administrative expenses made it costly for the Office of Indian Affairs to allot a reservation, those areas in highest demand by non-Indians should receive first attention.

To test this theory, Carlson estimated the date of allotment as a function of a number of variables that would reflect a larger demand for allotment. These variables included rainfall, percent of improved land in the state in which the reservation is located, and population density of the state in which the reservation is located. He concludes that

> A reservation in a region with less than 20 inches of rainfall per year was allotted 12.3 years later than a reservation located in the same state having more

TABLE 5.5   Farm Prices Per Acre

State	Nominal dollars			Real dollars (1880 prices)			Percentage rate of growth	
	1870	1880	1890	1870	1880	1890	1870-1880	1880-1890
Arkansas	4.20	6.10	8.00	3.10	6.10	9.70	97	58
Kansas	12.80	10.90	18.60	9.50	10.90	22.60	15	106
Missouri	14.50	13.50	20.40	10.70	13.50	24.80	25	84
Texas	2.60	4.70	7.80	1.90	4.70	9.50	143	102

Source: U.S. Bureau of the Census (1975).

than 20 inches of rainfall. . . . For the sample, the mean percentage of land improved was 43.44 percent, ranging from 1.7 percent in Arizona to 78.6 percent in Nebraska. The model predicts that . . . a reservation in a state like Arizona would be allotted 10.2 years later than a reservation in a state like Nebraska. The population density had a mean of 16.25, with a range from 1.5 in Wyoming to 48.9 in Michigan. The model predicts that a reservation in Michigan would be allotted 14.0 years earlier than a reservation in Wyoming. (Carlson, 1981, p. 44)

As with the Cherokee Outlet, these data support the theory that Indian policy was heavily dominated by non-Indian interest groups. Carlson, however, correctly notes that the theory that allotment timing "was shaped by non-Indian interests does not necessarily mean that the policy was a thinly disguised scheme for expropriating Indian lands" (1981, p. 44).

The argument is that the general program of allotting land in severalty was bent, pulled, and shaped by non-Indian economic interests. It is plausible to attribute the best of intentions for Indians on the part of reformers and the administrators in the Office of Indian Affairs who planned and instituted the allotment of Indian lands. (p. 44)

In other words, if the land was becoming more valuable, it also would have been in the Indians' interest to obtain title clear of political reallocation. This point seems especially true in light of the Alston and Spiller conclusion that Indian "property rights will be continually subject to change unless they are not subject to reallocation through legislation" (1992, p. 103).

A Switch in Time[8]

Though the demand pressures brought by land-hungry farmers influenced the timing of allotment, implementation was basically up to the Bureau of Indian Affairs whose job it was to survey the reservation land, assign parcels to individual Indians, and teach the Indians to become independent farmers. If it did its job, "when the process was complete there would be no more need for an Indian Office to manage relations with the Indians, for there would be no more identifiable Indians" (Prucha, 1984, p. 716).

And from the early speed with which allotment proceeded, it appeared that the BIA was doing its job. In particular, surplus lands were being sold off so rapidly that tribal lands declined from 119,375,930 acres in 1887 to 52,455,827 acres by 1900 (see Table 5.2).

> Year by year, in fact, the process of allotment was stepped up, and the surplus lands were rapidly transferred to the whites. . . . So successful did the process seem that the reformers looked forward to the day when government supervision over the Indians would disappear entirely and the Indians would all be absorbed into American Society. (Prucha, 1984, p. 671)

McChesney (1992) summarizes the effects of the speedy privatization of reservations:

> First, as always, the aim of the new policy was an end to any federal role in Indian affairs. In its "Declaration of Policy in the Administration of Indian Affairs" of April 1917, the Indian Office declared that the fee patent system "means the dawn of a new era in Indian Administration. . . . It means reduced appropriations by the Government and more self-respect and independence for the Indian. . . . It means in short, the beginning of the end of the Indian problem." Second, as Indian population declined and lands became privately owned and then were sold, Indian population and lands under the BIA administration began to decline. (pp. 114–115)

In sum, expectations were that allotment would lead to the end of the Indian bureaucracy.

Subsequent growth of the BIA suggests that the ringing of the death toll was premature. Rather than decline, the bureau continued to grow in both employment and budget, and other agencies responsible for education, housing, and welfare have increasingly devoted attention to the "Indian problem."

This result is hardly surprising as bureaucrats are highly unlikely to sit back and watch their mission and jobs wither. Niskanen has argued that budget maximization by bureaucracies makes them self-perpetuating, and more recent literature has contended that staff size, salaries, and power may all be a part of what bureaucrats maximize. But even if you ascribe benevolent motives to those trying to solve the Indian problem, it would be surprising to find the agency dismantled; there are always more problems to be solved, no matter how effective the agency has been at accomplishing its mission.

Evidence of the BIA's recognition that it might be working itself out of a job comes from the words of the Commissioner of Indian Affairs in 1906: "The grand total of the nation's wards will be diminished and at a growing ratio" (cited in McChesney, 1992, p. 127). But "instead of withering away according to the blueprint, the Indian Office vastly increased its involvement; it became a sort of real estate agent, handling a multitude of land transactions for individual Indians" (Prucha, 1984, p. 864). Schemeckebier concluded that "while the issuance of fee patents to allottees had decreased the number of Indians under the supervision of the Office of Indian Affairs, the control over the property and the fiscal affairs of individuals has resulted in an increase in the actual volume of work" (1927, p. 81).

The BIA found its *raison d'etre* with the passage of the Indian Reorganization Act in 1934. In addition to establishing tribal governments, the act ended the allotment process and froze most allotments for which fee patents had not been issued into perpetual trusteeship. McChesney (1992) explains the bureaucratic interest in the new policy:

> In its initial phases, allotment would serve bureaucrats' interest in greater budgets because it necessitated a growing Indian Office to administer the Dawes Act. . . . Ending allotments and freezing ownership for allottees still under federal trusteeship guaranteed that bureaucratic control would continue. Further, it meant that work would increase as the number of Indians on the reservation . . . would begin to increase—as in fact it did. . . . In short, one hy-

pothesis that explains the entire allotment episode is growth in agency budgets. (p. 125)

Every change in the sequence of allotment events from 1887 to 1934 led to an increase in the involvement of the federal government in Indian affairs, and each change can be explained by its ability to generate more work for the Indian bureaucracy. (p. 127)

Recalling Alston and Spiller's (1992) contention that citizen and congressional interests played an important role in Indian policy, it is important to ask why the BIA was so successful in adjusting Indian policy to maximize its budgets. To be sure, whites were interested in access to reservation land, but that interest had waned by the 1920s because "the value of Western land fell with the steep decline in livestock and agricultural prices" and because "the best Indian lands would already have been allotted" (McChesney, 1992, p. 123). This took some pressure off Congress to leave reservation lands open for non-Indian acquisition and therefore increased the relative influence of the bureaucracy, which, as mentioned above, was both a demander and a supplier of policy. The agency lobbied Congress to end allotment and to provide additional funding so it could carry out its new mission.

The budget evidence mustered by McChesney is convincing. Not only did BIA budgets grow but that growth was significantly increased by both the number of allotments and the acreage allotted. But the rate of budget increase attributable to allotments declined over time, giving the BIA an incentive to find an alternative policy that would sustain bureaucratic growth. The Indian Reorganization Act, which began during the New Deal, provided the policy change that has driven the agency even to the present. McChesney (1992) summarizes his findings, noting that an explanation

consistent with the entire allotment episode is that its real beneficiaries were Eastern and Western whites, politicians, and the Indian Office. By 1920, however, only the Indian bureaucrats had interests strongly affected by allotment, and those interests dictated an end to privatization. Initial allotment and subsequent changes that augmented Indian owner-ship worked to the benefit of the bureaucrats by enlarging their budgets. But as the amount of privat-ized land increased, these budget gains could not continue. Eventually privatization was stopped—which caused budgets to increase further. (p. 135)

Conclusion

There are, of course, arguments that the allotment experiment was a failure because it transferred so much land to whites, but there is no systematic evidence to test this proposition. Cer-tainly vast amounts of land were transferred to whites, but by itself this is not prima facie evidence that Indians were left worse off. If land was taken without compensation, there is no doubt that Indians were disadvantaged. To determine the impact of voluntary sales, we would have to know the sale price relative to the value of the land to Indians had it been retained by them.[9] In the absence of this evidence, there is one conclu-sion that is clear from the allotment episode: Rather than promoting self-reliance and self-determination for today's Indi-ans, late nineteenth- and early twentieth-century policy left reservation Indians entangled in a bureaucratic quagmire where they continue to be wards of the state.

Notes

1. Carlson notes that "the cession of surplus lands to the government was to be approved by the tribe, although in practice the government had a strong position in such negotiations. The role of the tribes was reduced further in 1903 when the courts held that tribal approval was not necessary for the disposal of surplus lands. The proceeds from the land sales were held in trust for the tribe" (1981, p. 10).

2. See Yandle (1993) for a discussion of this alliance.

3. This does not necessarily mean that Indians were worse off. Indeed, giving them private ownership of land may have released them from the shackles of the bureaucracy. Even if they later sold the land to non-Indians, they may have been better off with the more liquid form of capital.

4. The title for this section and the data are taken from Alston and Spiller (1992).

5. This use of the army in Indian policy is consistent with the story told in Chapter 4.

6. Alston and Spiller (1992) explain how the purchase price of $1.25 per acre was determined: "This low price reflects the Cherokees' lack of property rights and bargaining power, as well as the heterogenous composition of the Appropriations Committee. The president and the Eastern legislators had an incentive in keeping the sale price low, whereas the political agents of the agricultural interests had an incentive to get the price high enough to avoid negation of the sale through judicial review" (p. 101).

7. The data for this section are taken from Carlson (1981, ch. 2).

8. The hypothesis here was developed and tested by McChesney (1992).

9. For a more complete discussion of arguments against privatization of reservation lands see McChesney (1992, pp. 118–122).

CHAPTER 6

The Legacy of Allotment[1]

Since being relegated to reservations in the latter part of the nineteenth century, Indians have found themselves subject to a wide range of federal policies. The white man's government assumed the role of trustee for the Indian wards with the Bureau of Indian Affairs acting as the government's agent. Initial federal policies were aimed at assimilating the Indians into an agrarian economy by allotting parcels of land to individual Indians in an attempt to develop private ownership of reservations and the incentives therein. Later policies, however, halted the privatization process, and even later ones attempted to terminate the system of reservations. Most recently the rhetoric of Indian policy has focused on self-determination by Indians on reservations.

Whatever the policies, the economic outcome is clear: Indians generally have remained at the bottom of the economic ladder. Traditional explanations for the lack of economic growth among Indians have typically focused on insufficient access to capital markets, low levels of education and poor work attitudes, and small endowments of natural resources. Following standard economic development strategies, governmental policies have attempted to augment the capital stock on reservations. Special loan funds, subsidized interest, and direct federal investment have been among the investment strategies. In addition to augmenting physical capital, efforts have been made to enhance Indian human capital. Primary and secondary education, college scholarships and, most recently, tribal colleges have been the focus of this investment. To add to the stock of natural resources, efforts have been made to acquire additional tribal land, and litigation continues to obtain water rights for Indian agriculture. Whether the efforts in each of these areas has been sufficient is open for debate,[2] but it is clear that there has been little change in economic conditions on reservations.

To this list of possible explanations for the lack of development on reservations must be added the institutional environment. Trosper concluded that "land tenure and other institutional problems underlie Indian difficulties attaining the operating scale of whites in ranching" and called for further research to "investigate the nature of these relationships rather than focus upon Indian abilities and goals" (1978, p. 514). To date, however, few have answered Trosper's call.

In this chapter, I will examine one particular aspect of Indian institutions, land tenure on reservations. After an initial period when Indians were left to develop their own land tenure arrangements, the federal government played a pivotal role in molding land institutions. The result of this bureaucratic control is a mosaic of land tenure institutions that fit into three basic tenure categories:

- *fee simple,* under which individual Indians and non-Indians own the land, can determine its use, and can transfer it to new owners without BIA supervision;

- *individual trust,* under which land has been allotted to individual Indians but remains held in trust by the BIA as a check on individual decisions; and

- *tribal trust,* under which land is owned by the tribe but held in trust by the BIA as a check on tribal decisions.

Because these three tenure arrangements have very different implications for agricultural productivity, they offer an excellent opportunity for measuring the impact of ownership institutions on reservations.

After considering Indian land tenure and farming prior to the Dawes Act, the legacy of allotment is measured using cross-section data on land tenure and agricultural output from large western reservations. Again, the story that emerges is that Indians were quite adaptable prior to federally imposed tenure arrangements and that trusteeship under the BIA has raised the costs of organizing agricultural productivity sufficiently to thwart production.

Learning to Farm[3]

Between the time when many Indians were placed on reservations and when allotment policies were effectively implemented, Indians were mostly left to their own devices. Without abundant buffalo and without much government support, tribes had little choice but to provide for themselves with the resources at hand. To do so required institutional changes as significant as those that accompanied adaptation to the horse culture. This led Josephy to conclude that "particularly those who had traditionally been nomadic hunters and gatherers, could not or would not become farmers overnight; they had neither the cultural background nor the necessary training" (1968, p. 351). Similarly, Hurt argued that "only the most agricultural tribes, such as the Cherokee, showed much aptitude and success in farming once removed west of the Mississippi River. The tribes that had no agricultural traditions, such as the Sioux, found the sedentary farming life culturally unacceptable" (1987, p. 230). Where there was an agricultural tradition, however, "the Indian concept of land tenure enabled various villages to make the best possible use of the [reservation] land in order to meet their own specific needs" (p. 75).

But the theory and the evidence regarding institutional change presented in Chapter 3 suggest that even the hunter-gatherers might have adapted to their new conditions. Recall that prior to the horse, many of the Sioux bands on the eastern border of the Plains had practiced some form of settled agriculture but became mostly nomadic equestrian hunters. For these hunters, the leap back into sedentary agricultural may not have been so great. In fact, Carlson finds that the Yankton Dakota (Sioux) Indians, whose reservation was established in the late

1850s, experienced a "growth of farming by individual Indians so that by 1878 farming was conducted by 'each man to himself on his own plot of ground'" (1992, p. 73). Similarly, the Santee Sioux, the Yakima, and the Flathead, "all had recognized individual property rights in land before allotment" (p. 74). "Such claims had sufficient legal status that on the Flathead Reservation in the early 1880s individuals were compensated for improvements in land when a railroad was granted a right-of-way through their land" (p. 73).

Indian cattle ranching prior to allotment also evolved as the costs and benefits of adapting new institutions changed. Given economies of scale in grazing and a tradition of private ownership of horses, it made sense to have individual ownership of the livestock and common ownership of the land.[4] On the Blackfeet Reservation in Montana, "the tradition of individual ownership was so well established that Indians resisted government efforts to establish common herds from 1910 to 1920. According to John C. Ewers, 'the fullbloods, who had always considered livestock in terms of individual possessions, showed little interest in the tribal herd. They acted as if it belonged to someone else'" (Carlson, 1992, p. 74). Based on this evidence, Carlson observes:

> Once a tribe was confined to a reservation, it needed to find a land tenure system suitable to the new environment. On the closed reservations, the system that evolved was one of use rights. Typically, the [BIA] agent and members of a tribe recognized an individual's title to animals and, where farming was practiced, a family's claim to the land it worked. . . . What is remarkable is how similar this system of land tenure was to that which existed among agricultural tribes before being confined to reservations. (p. 73)

Under these tenure arrangements, Indians throughout Indian Country were discovering how to farm in their new economic environment. Given their agricultural heritage and their experience with trading, it is not surprising that the Five Civilized Tribes adapted first. Wessel finds that by 1877 these tribes "produced over 69 percent of the wheat grown on Indian reservations, 81 percent of the corn, and over 43 percent of the vegetables" (1976, p. 17). But once the buffalo were gone from the Plains, Indians from nonagricultural traditions began to cultivate their land. Acreage cultivated by all Indians except those in the Five Civilized Tribes

> rose from less that 117,267 acres in 1875 to 379,974 acres by 1896. Similarly, a five-year moving average of the output of grain . . . shows that Indian grain output also grew . . . by 5.5 percent per year from 1875 to 1895 and by 3.1 percent for the whole period from 1875 to 1904. . . . These data show that after 1875, many Indians who were members of tribes without extensive agricultural traditions did try to become farmers. (Carlson, 1992, p. 75)

The 1900 U.S. Census concluded that "notwithstanding the numerous difficulties, there has been steady progress toward civilization in the past decade on most reservations. A number of tribes are now peaceable, self-supporting agriculturists, wearing citizens' clothing, and able to speak the English language" (U.S. Bureau of the Census, 1900, p. 717).

On the reservations too arid to cultivate without irrigation, cattle ranching was increasing prior to allotment. The 1900 U.S. Census stated that Indians on the Standing Rock Reservation "have begun to realize that their support must come from their cattle, and they give them great care, stock raising being even now their principal pursuit, although most of them grow a few small crops in addition to cutting large quantities of wild grass" (U.S. Bureau of the Census, 1900, p. 722). For the unallotted reservations in 1900, "the average number of head per family ranged from 16 to nearly 40. These figures do not indicate that Indian cattlemen were self-sufficient, but they do indicate a healthy beginning" (Carlson, 1981, p. 123).

This evidence confirms that the Indians who adapted to the often harsh conditions of the Plains and to the introduction of the horse were equally capable of adapting to agriculture on reservations. Certainly there was resistance to agriculture, but as Linton notes, "It is an open question how far this resistance stemmed from the aboriginal culture and how far from the fact that most of the lands assigned in severalty were unsuited for farming and insufficient in amount to support individual families" (1942, p. 54). As with other land laws, such as the Homestead Act,[5] top-down federal policies to establish property rights often ignore the time- and place-specific circumstances that determine efficient institutions. "The allotment episode and most policy since have ignored the ability of Indians to adapt their institutions, but evidence of successful reservation agriculture before allotment provides ground for optimism regarding self-determination" (Carlson, 1992, p. 81).

Reservation Land Tenure Under Allotment

Contrary to the notion that reservations belong to Indian tribes, much of the land is privately owned in fee simple tenure nearly identical to private land outside the reservation. This fee simple land owned by both Indians and non-Indians provides a benchmark against which we can measure the impact of alternative institutions on agricultural productivity.

In contrast to fee simple land owned by both Indians and non-Indians, Indian Land includes only that portion of the reservation owned by the tribe or individual Indians but held in trust by the Bureau of Indian Affairs. Ostensibly under the control of tribes or individual Indians, use of these trust lands is overseen by the BIA. Generally, under its trust authority, the BIA grants or denies permission to change land use, approves lease arrangements, and agrees to capital improvements. The question addressed here is whether this added layer of bureaucracy inhibits agricultural productivity.

As shown previously in Table 5.2, millions of acres of land were transferred from tribal control to individuals. Between 1871 and 1983, almost 70 million acres fell into individual Indian and non-Indian hands with only 10 million of those acres held in trust by the BIA.[6] Of more than 54 million acres of Indian Land in 1987, 77 percent was tribal trust, 20 percent was individual trust, and 2 percent was government owned.[7] In the set of 39 large reservations, 47 percent of reservation acreage is in fee simple ownership (owned by either Indians or non-Indians) that is not subject to BIA or tribal authority. The data in Table 6.1 show the number of total reservation acres (Indian Country) as well as the number of acres of tribal trust, individual trust, and fee simple land for these 39 large reservations. This mosaic of land tenure can be traced to the Dawes Act of 1887.

As discussed in Chapter 5, the dominant federal goal at the time reservations were being established was to assimilate Indians into white society by promoting agricultural development of reservation land through the General Allotment (Dawes) Act of 1887.[8] Generally, an Indian family could claim 160 acres, which, like acreage limits under the homestead acts, was too little for an efficient farm in the arid regions of the West.

Allotment had three major effects on reservation land tenure. First, it broke up contiguous tribal landholdings by allocating land to individual Indians and allowing settlement of tribal lands by non-Indians. Second, as whites settled tribal lands and individual allottees gained fee simple title to their allotments, land owned in fee simple became interspersed with land held under trusteeship. Third, when the allotment policy ended in 1934, more than 10 million allotted acres, nearly 20 percent of total Indian Lands, were left in the peculiar legal status of individual trust, that is, owned by individual Indians but held in trust by the BIA.

Fee simple ownership of land is a nearly absolute right to use and alienate a parcel of land. According to *Black's Law Dictionary* (Black, 1983), "an absolute or fee simple estate is one in which the owner is entitled to the entire property, with unconditional power of disposition during his life, and descending to his heirs and legal representatives upon his death intestate" (p. 317). Fee simple lands are "private" lands that do not fall under the trust authority of the BIA and hence are essentially the same as fee simple lands outside Indian Country.[9] As the data in Table 6.1 show, fee simple lands constitute a substantial fraction of Indian Country.

Fee simple lands came into existence on reservations when Indian allotments were released from trusteeship or when surplus lands were homesteaded. The former occurred automatically after 25 years unless the allottee requested to have the trust period extended. Allottees could have gained fee simple ownership earlier if in the secretary of the interior's judgment the allottee was deemed "competent and capable of managing his or her affairs at any time . . . and thereafter all restrictions as to sale, encumbrance, or taxation of said land

TABLE 6.1 Acreage in Various Ownership Classifications for Selected Reservations, 1987

State Reservation	Total[a]	Tribal Trust[b]	Individual Trust[c]	Fee Simple
Washington				
Colville	1,367,761	1,028,339	39,940	299,475
Yakima	1,402,469	918,544	222,937	260,965
Oregon				
Umatilla	174,800	19,273	68,612	86,792
Warm Springs	659,012	587,794	51,105	15,441
Idaho				
Fort Hall	522,600	269,655	220,313	0
Coeur d'Alene	345,750	22,470	39,237	284,043
Nez Perce	805,815	36,949	47,244	721,612
Montana				
Blackfeet	1,546,950	312,879	628,822	605,113
Crow	2,347,177	414,263	1,095,373	836,140
Flathead	1,287,941	609,365	42,640	635,213
Rocky Boys	127,235	108,325	0	18,910
Fort Peck	2,162,288	395,703	510,093	1,246,492
Northern Cheyenne	471,415	321,363	115,585	34,466
Wyoming				
Wind River	2,195,940	1,794,758	93,413	306,473
North Dakota				
Fort Berthold	797,505	70,997	351,469	374,875
Standing Rock	2,306,098	356,037	441,211	1,508,850
Fort Totten	255,203	16,228	36,635	202,172
South Dakota				
Cheyenne River	2,872,342	959,687	444,901	1,435,993
Crow Creek	310,293	65,018	60,425	184,850
Lower Brule	245,956	106,135	22,597	112,694
Pine Ridge	2,779,200	708,559	1,070,058	998,263
Rosebud Sioux	1,624,202[d]	529,575	429,575	664,631
Yankton	406,045	16,706	19,852	369,487
Sisseton	978,465	17,544	90,518	870,112
Nebraska				
Omaha	186,591	9,596	17,196	159,799

(continued)

TABLE 6.1 Acreage in Various Ownership Classifications for Selected Reservations, 1987 *(continued)*

State Reservation	Total[a]	Tribal Trust[b]	Individual Trust[c]	Fee Simple
Santee	111,844	6,943	2,415	102,486
Winnebago	111,876	4,321	23,282	84,273
Kansas				
Kickapoo	13,696	3,659	3,124	6,913
Arizona				
Colorado River	269,918[d]	264,048	5,870	0
Gila River	347,474	269,128	97,642	18
Nevada				
Duck Valley	286,816[d]	289,819	0	0
Walker River	323,406	313,690	8,572	8,572
Utah				
Goshute	109,293[d]	109,133	80	0
Uintah & Ouray	4,337,393	1,007,278	14,318	3,375,795
New Mexico				
Isleto Pueblo	211,981	211,037	0	36
Colorado				
Southern Ute	629,313	307,562	2,408	316,241
Ute Mountain	579,073	307,562	8,578	0
Oklahoma				
Osage	1,435,114	734	168,119	1,264,895
Minnesota				
Fond Du Lac	78,958	4,701	16,185	57,947

Notes: [a] Total acres are estimated from reservation maps using a computerized planimeter. For reservations where all land is held in trust, total acres are calculated as the sum of tribal and individual trust. [b] Tribal trust and individual trust acreage is taken from the U.S. Department of Interior, Bureau of Indian Affairs (1987) Natural Resources Information Service (NRIS) data. [c] Fee simple lands are the difference between total acres and total NRIS acres. [d] In cases where there is no fee simple ownership, total acreage is calculated as the NRIS estimate of total Indian land. Total acres do not necessarily equal the sum of the three classes of ownership because government and other owners are not included.

shall be removed and said land shall not be liable to the satisfaction of any debt contract prior to the issuing of such patent" (Getches & Wilkinson, 1986, p. 561). Once released from trust status, allotted lands could be freely alienated by sale or inheritance to either Indians or non-Indians, substantially reducing control by the tribe or the Bureau of Indian Affairs.

When the allotment era ended with the Indian Reorganization Act in 1934, roughly 10 million acres of allotted land had not been released from trust status. Because the 1934 act prevented the alienation of trust land, these allotments could not be sold out of trust status, taxed, or subjected to legal encumbrance such as liens or mortgages. All of these constraints were binding even though title was legally held by the allottee.[10] In addition, restrictions were placed on the way individual trust lands could be passed on to heirs.

Under the 1887 General Allotment Act, if an allottee died before obtaining fee simple title, the allotment could not be willed but had to pass to the heirs according to state rules of inheritance where the land was located. This was later changed to allow estate inheritance through a will, although the will may be set aside if the decedent's family is not included (25 U.S.C.A. Sec. 348, 373, [1964]).[11] These heirship restrictions generally mean that each allotment is inherited by a large number of individuals, each of whom has a share in land use decisions. Because of these heirship provisions, "reservation allotments are held by so many owners in common that the Indians are helpless to make effective use of their property. Unless this pattern can be reversed, all Indian allotments inevitably will have an astronomical number of owners" (Williams 1970–1971, pp. 710–711). By 1960, 12 million acres of allotted lands were in heirship status with half of that owned by six or more heirs.

Tribal trust lands differ from individual trust lands because title is held by an organized tribe subject to allocation by the tribal governing unit and to the trust authority of the federal government.[12] As shown in Table 5.2, the shift in ownership from allotted to tribal in recent years reflects the efforts of tribes to consolidate and enlarge their landholdings.

Management of tribal lands varies considerably by reservation depending on the collective decision-making mechanism used by the tribe. In most cases, a tribal council is the general governing body that ultimately decides how tribal lands will be used. How well these councils enhance the welfare of Indians depends mostly on constitutional and cultural constraints.

Land Tenure and the Costs of Organizing Agriculture

The types of land tenure described here must be considered a factor in Indian economic development. Because most western reservations are rural and have large land bases, sustained economic development is tied to efficient natural resource management. Agricultural productivity particularly depends on the costs of combining labor and capital with land. The higher the costs of organizing these inputs, the lower agricultural productivity, all else being equal. Because these organizational costs vary systematically with the different types of land tenure, agricultural productivity would also be expected to vary systematically.

Fee Simple Tenure

Fee simple land tenure is a norm against which other tenures will be measured because fee simple landowners have nearly exclusive use rights and face the fewest constraints on alienation. Furthermore, because the land can be sold or otherwise encumbered, fee simple ownership allows the landowner to use land as a guarantee (collateral) in the capital market. With fewer constraints on contracting, land owned in fee simple will be subject to lower costs of organizing inputs compared with other land tenures. It is therefore reasonable to expect that fee simple owners will employ the optimal amounts of land, labor, and capital and maximize the net value of output.

Individual Trust Tenure

The bureaucratic regulations placed on individual trust lands increase the costs of management decisions compared to fee simple land. First, and perhaps most important, the restriction on alienation or other encumbrances constrains the use of land as collateral in the capital market. Banks making loans cannot easily sell the land to collect on defaulted loans, and even the government cannot take the land in return for delinquent taxes. Given the constraints on alienation, the capital deficiency recognized by Trosper (1978) is more appropriately viewed as the result of trust restrictions.[13]

Second, the cost of alienating land also prevents the land from being held in its optimal configuration, thus lowering the value of the land and agricultural productivity. When allotments were made, they tended to be small, usually less than 320 acres. In nearly all types of modern agriculture, this parcel size is too small for optimal use with other inputs. In Montana, for instance, Blackfeet tribe members were allotted 320 acres. Today, in this region, the size of the average farm is greater than 1500 acres.

Third, the fractionation of individual trust land resulting from heirship increases the costs of establishing a clear owner and manager who can control land use decisions and reap the benefits of good management. As ownership becomes more divided, the costs of coordinating production and selling or leasing land increase dramatically.[14] The story one allottee told the House Committee on Interior and Insular Affairs is illustrative of the problems that arise with fractionation:

> My sister's allotment was 80 acres. She dies and my dad, a white man, was willed the land. He dies and all his children fell heir. His share was 13440/20160. We had that probated in court—four children share is 960/20160, and cousins one share 270/20160, one share 305/20160, five shares 128/20160, one share 320/20160, one share 140/20160, seven shares 35/20160 and these last seven are no relation only that this man was once a brother-in-law and they are the ones that won't sign so that we can have a 100 percent signers [the requirement for sale or lease of allotments]. (U.S. House of Representatives, 1960, p. 463)

Land ownership record keeping becomes more complicated each day because of the heirship problem as this BIA report suggests.

There are over 200,000 surface tracts of individually

owned trust land with an average tract ownership of 10 undivided interest owners. This means there are over 2,000,000 separate undivided interests to keep track of. Ownership in some tracts is so complicated that owners own an undivided interest in which the common denominator is in the quintillionths. If such tracts were leased, some undivided-interest owners would receive a fraction of a penny. This kind of ownership either makes it impossible to develop such tracts or severely restricts the development since all owners have to be contacted. (U.S. Department of the Interior, 1981, p. 104)

The combination of the coordination problem resulting from heirship and the constraints on alienation should lower agricultural output on individual trust lands relative to the fee simple lands.

Tribal Trust Tenure

Tribal trust tenure also is expected to put constraints on organizing inputs that will restrict agricultural productivity relative to fee simple lands. As with individual trust lands, it is difficult to use tribal lands as collateral in capital markets except through programs of the federal government where eligibility for loans is generally less restrictive than in commercial credit markets. The collateral problem, however, is likely to be less severe for tribes than for individuals because tribes often have other alienable resources that can be used as collateral.

More crucial to productivity on tribal trust lands is the extent to which tribal governance structures are able to prevent the power of tribal government from being used to encourage wealth transfers as opposed to enhanced productivity. Instead of maximizing the income stream from tribal lands, government officials could allow political patronage to determine land use. For example, Libecap and Johnson conclude that the politics of the Navajo Tribal Council and its grazing committees have essentially legislated "a common property condition for the range" (1980, p. 83), wherein access is open to all tribal members and overuse occurs.

The impact of tribal control on agricultural productivity is more difficult to predict because there is such a variety of explicit decision rules and implicit cultural norms. If a tribe had a history of agriculture and the associated land tenure institutions, it is more likely that land will be put to productive use. Also, if the tribal population is small relative to the number of tribally controlled acres, tribal council decisions will have a greater impact per capita and therefore are more likely to be scrutinized by members, thus leading to more productive land use.

Cornell and Kalt (1992b) have asked "what can tribes do" to promote reservation development and conclude that

> unless there is a fit between the culture of the community and the structure and powers of its governing institutions, those institutions may be seen as illegitimate, their ability to regulate and organize the development process will be undermined, and development will be blocked. Without a match between culture and governing institutions, tribal government cannot consistently do its basic job: creating and sustaining the "rules of the game" that development in any society requires. (p. 10)

Quantifying tribal institutions is quite difficult, but comparing agricultural productivity on tribal trust lands with fee simple lands gives an indication of how effective tribal institutions are at harnessing the power of government for productivity rather than for wealth transfers.

Implications for Agricultural Output

The general hypothesis tested here is that, all else being equal, the *gross* value of agricultural output per acre will be lower for individual trust and tribal trust land relative to fee simple land because tenure constraints influence the costs of organizing agricultural production.[15] Because the costs of organizing production under fee simple tenure are lower than under individual or tribal trust tenure, fee simple owner's choice of a land, labor, and capital mix is taken as approximately optimal. If that is so, trust tenures should exhibit lower productivity compared to fee simple tenure for several reasons. First, trust constraints raise the cost of capital by restricting alienation. Because trust land cannot be easily encumbered, private lending institutions are reluctant to loan funds for investment on trust lands. Second, trust constraints reduce the incentive for individuals to monitor land management to the extent that the proceeds are shared among the collective of heirs or the collective of tribal members. Because each heir or tribal member receives only a small fraction of total output, any management contribution he or she makes that increases output will be shared with the group, thus reducing his or her incentive to improve land management. To the extent that tribal governance structures can overcome the problems of collective management, agricultural output on tribal trust lands should be higher.

The reduction in output caused by too little application of capital and management inputs is exacerbated by the problem of sub-optimally sized farming units, especially on individual trust land. When ownership patterns do not coincide with the optimal size production unit, lease or sale is required to consolidate landholdings in the appropriate configuration. If parcels could be bought, sold, or leased, this problem would be overcome through market transactions, but restrictions on alienation inhibit such exchanges. Fee simple land can easily be alienated, but the BIA must supervise and approve all leases of Indian land, thus raising the costs of organizing optimal farming units. Because allotments were generally small compared to today's optimal farm size, the scale of farming on restricted fee lands will be too small, contributing to a reduction in output per acre.

Evidence from Reservation Agriculture

Trust lands tend to be used in relatively low valued uses, such as grazing, rather than in higher valued uses such as row crops, small grains, and horticulture. The Natural Resources Information System (U.S. Department of the Interior, Bureau of Indian Affairs, 1987) summary for all reservations shows that 82 percent of Indian land was in grazing earning $3.48 per acre. In contrast, 1 percent was in row crops earning $380 per acre, 2 percent in small grains earning $91 per acre, 1 percent in forage-hay-pasture earning $145 per acre, and one-tenth of 1 percent in horticulture earning $497 per acre. The incentive to develop land can be examined by understanding the constraints associated with each of the three dominant tenure systems in Indian Country.[16]

A more systematic test of the impact of tenure can be conducted by using data from the BIA's Natural Resource Information System (1987). This source contains information on acres devoted to a variety of land use classes, acres under Indian and non-Indian management, land quality, and value of products grown on Indian land for a large number of reservations. By combining these data for 1987 with data from the 1987 U.S. Agricultural Census (U.S. Bureau of the Census 1989) for counties encompassing the reservations, it is possible to compare agricultural output for Indian trust land with fee simple land for 39 large western reservations.[17]

The estimate of the value of agricultural output from Indian land includes row crops, small grains, forage-hay-pasture, horticulture, native hay, and grazing. To obtain a per-acre value, this total value is divided by Indian acres with agricultural potential.[18] The data in Table 6.2 compare the value of output per acre for individual trust and tribal trust land with the value per acre of cultivated crops (excluding grazing and cattle production) grown on all farms in surrounding counties. Because the BIA collects no data for fee simple land on reservations, the value per acre for fee simple land is a weighted average for all farms in the counties encompassing the reservation. Weights are the estimated percentage of the reservation within each county.

The data in Table 6.2 report these output values and ratios for each reservation in the sample. The ratio of trust land output to fee simple land output shows that trust lands produce only about half the value of fee simple lands on a per acre basis. On average, trust lands are about half as productive as fee simple lands, and the difference is statistically significant.[19]

To determine the extent to which the value of reservation output will decline as the fraction of the reservation land subject to trust constraints rises, it is necessary to control for other variables using regression analysis. The value of reservation output is the sum of the value of output from individual and tribal trust land and the value of output from fee simple land on reservations[20] divided by Indian acres with agricultural potential plus all fee simple acres. Note that the value of reservation output per acre measures the value of *reservation* output per acre rather than the value of *trust* output per acre. The value of fee simple output is simply the value of output per acre for fee simple land.[21] The ratio of the value of reservation output to the value of fee simple output will equal one if all the reservation is held in fee or if there are no differences in output for the three tenure categories.

By comparing output on trust land and fee simple land within a given reservation, many other factors that could affect output are taken into account. In other words, differential affects due to temperature and moisture wash out since weather is approximately constant across the reservation. Similarly, the cost of farm inputs (other than capital) should be approximately equal to all input users within a reservation regardless of tenure.

The impact of trust tenure on the value of reservation agricultural output was computed by estimating the variations in the ratio of the value of reservation output to fee simple output that are caused by the fraction of reservation land held in individual trust tenure, by the fraction held in tribal trust tenure, and by other variables such as human capital, physical capital, and farm size.[22] Holding these other variables constant, the per-acre value of agricultural output was found to be 85 to 90 percent lower on tribal trust land than on fee simple land and 30 to 40 percent lower on individual trust land than on fee simple land.[23] The magnitude of these numbers supports the contention that trust constraints on Indian land reduce agricultural productivity. The inability to alienate trust lands, the difficulty in using trust land as collateral, and the transaction costs resulting from multiple owners of small parcels all make it difficult to maximize productivity. The results are especially significant on tribal trust land and suggest that tribal governance institutions have not significantly offset the difficulties of making collective decisions that promote productivity.

There are two other variables that might explain the differences in agricultural productivity, land quality and water availability. Unfortunately, data on land quality in the Natural Resources Information System were not complete for the full

TABLE 6.2 Average Value of Agricultural Output Per Acre, 1987

State Reservation	Trust Value / County	Trust	County Value
Washington			
Colville	$292.19	$7.15	0.02
Yakima	857.45	24.72	0.03
Oregon			
Umatilla	143.36	43.06	0.30
Warm Springs	174.36	2.01	0.01
Idaho			
Fort Hall	132.64	102.79	0.77
Coeur d'Alene	115.80	203.05	1.75
Nez Perce	101.53	87.40	0.79
Montana			
Blackfeet	45.10	11.61	0.26
Crow	46.17	22.06	0.48
Flathead	44.69	9.46	0.21
Rocky Boys	39.54	19.64	0.50
Fort Peck	27.33	13.80	0.50
Northern Cheyenne	40.41	7.50	0.19
Wyoming			
Wind River	54.80	3.76	0.07
North Dakota			
Fort Berthold	28.83	16.52	0.57
Standing Rock	18.49	19.86	1.07
Fort Totten	41.00	15.22	0.37
South Dakota			
Cheyenne River	21.21	0.00	0.00
Crow Creek	39.35	39.68	1.01
Lower Brule	38.80	39.26	1.01
Pine Ridge	28.32	10.12	0.36
Rosebud Sioux	24.92	11.19	0.45
Yankton	45.50	42.93	0.94
Sisseton	53.01	37.22	0.70

(continued)

TABLE 6.2   Average Value of Agricultural Output
Per Acre, 1987 *(continued)*

State Reservation	Trust Value/ County	Trust	County Value
Nebraska			
Omaha	100.23	156.34	1.55
Santee	38.99	35.73	0.92
Winnebago	97.79	154.86	1.58
Kansas			
Kickapoo	98.16	47.75	0.49
Arizona			
Colorado River	1,152.61	266.83	0.23
Gila River	577.00	239.90	0.42
Nevada			
Duck Valley	95.09	6.06	0.06
Walker River	94.18	3.77	0.04
Utah			
Goshute	37.39	1.71	0.05
Uintah-Ouray	24.04	8.02	0.33
New Mexico			
Isleto Pueblo	163.94	4.85	0.03
Colorado			
Southern Ute	21.02	17.72	0.84
Oklahoma			
Osage	18.47	30.63	1.66
Minnesota			
Fond Du Lac	25.99	12.58	0.48
n	39	39	39
Mean	130.18	45.57	0.54
Standard Deviation	230.83	67.29	0.49

Source: The values were calculated by using a weighted-average of average cropland value per acre for the counties encompassing each reservation. Cropland values and cropland acreage for the counties were taken from the U.S. Bureau of the Census (1989). The weights for each county value were the percentage of the reservation acreage found in a given county.

sample; only 13 reservations in the sample have had land capability inventories completed. Land capability is classified by the Soil Conservation Service according to its agricultural capacity. Generally, the top four classes are suitable for arable agricultural, and the percentage for each of these is listed in Table 6.3.

TABLE 6.3   Percentage of Land in Top Four Capability Classes

State Reservation	Percentage county	Percentage trust	County quality / trust quality
Idaho			
Ft. Hall	39.67	64.25	0.62
Montana			
Blackfeet	49.65	50.20	0.99
Crow	33.55	48.50	0.69
Rocky Boys	34.80	76.30	0.46
Northern Cheyenne	40.49	35.45	1.14
Wyoming			
Wind River	55.49	9.10	6.10
North Dakota			
Standing Rock	6.27	50.70	0.12
South Dakota			
Cheyenne River	37.40	33.10	1.13
Crow Creek	44.50	70.50	0.63
Pine Ridge	33.38	37.80	0.88
Rosebud	40.86	63.10	0.65
Yankton	40.45	86.25	0.47
Arizona			
Gila River	41.87	20.96	2.00
n	13	13	13
Mean	38.34	49.71	1.22
Standard Deviation	11.02	21.43	1.47

Sources: U.S. Department of the Interior, Bureau of Indian Affairs (1987); and U.S. Department of Agriculture, Soil Conservation Service (1970).

Contrary to what might be expected, the ratio of trust land in the top four categories to fee simple land in the same categories is 1.22 for these 13 reservations.[24] This ratio does not suggest that reservations are made up of the worst land in the area and therefore that land quality is the main cause of differences between the value of output on trust and fee simple lands. When land quality as reported in the sub-sample is used as a control in the regression analysis, it does not prove to be a statistically significant variable in explaining differences across reservations in the ratio of the value of reservation output to the value of fee simple output. A more likely impact of poor land capability is that it requires additional capital investment to mitigate the effects of lower land quality. If so, the problem is that trust constraints raise the cost of obtaining capital investment for Indian lands and thus make it more difficult to overcome quality differences. Whatever the data limitations inherent in this approach, it seems clear that trust tenure does make a difference to agricultural productivity.

It is even more difficult to determine the impact of water availability on productivity. While it is true that Indian lands often lack irrigation facilities, this may again be a capital constraint. Indians can purchase water rights, though the inability to borrow against their land may make the capital costs prohibitive. Moreover, many tribes are winning large water settlements under the Winters Doctrine, and recent settlements have included additional capital to deliver the water to Indian lands.[25]

Land Tenure and Forestry

Further support for the conclusion that trust tenure raises the costs of organizing inputs and reduces resource productivity is provided by Krepps' study of American Indian forestry. He hypothesized that tribal control of Indian forestry resources would result in higher worker productivity, lower costs, and higher incomes relative to BIA control because tribal control "shifts the onus of accountability for tribal forestry onto the tribes themselves without necessitating any increase in federal appropriations" (1992, pp. 181–182). Indians can get control of their forestry resource through Public Law 638, the Indian

Self-Determination and Education Assistance Act, passed by Congress in 1975. This law allows tribes to contract with the government to undertake responsibility for tribal operations formerly under control of the BIA as trustee. "By participating in the 638 program, a tribe takes over one or more of these aspects itself and receives the concomitant funding to dispense as it sees fit in the task" (Krepps 1992, p. 181). In the case of tribal forestry, Krepps (1992) found that 49 of 75 tribes in his sample participated in the 638 forestry program, in some cases to the extent of taking total control of tribal forestry. Participation in this program has led to the replacement of 4,000 BIA forestry workers with tribal workers, and not surprisingly, generated opposition to the program within the bureaucracy.

The impact of tribal control on forest productivity was measured using regression analysis to account for differences between the annual harvest level and the annual allowable cut (AAC).[26] Krepps believes that the extent to which the annual harvest level is less than the AAC depends on "four primary factors: the amount of timber available for sale, the maintenance efforts of low-skilled workers, the marketing efforts of high-skilled workers, and the internal rate of time preference . . . of the forest's owner" (1992, p. 185). His statistical analysis shows that the addition of "tribal high-skilled labor" increases harvest by 24,000 board feet (bf) per worker per year, while the addition of "BIA high-skilled labor" reduces harvest by 14,000 bf per worker per year. While additional "BIA low-skilled labor" increases harvest by 40 bf per year per worker, additional "tribal low-skilled labor" is 75 percent more effective. "This differential labor productivity provides a compelling rebuttal of the argument that tribes cannot manage their own resources" (p. 188).

Because the price received for timber is a function of marketing skills and incentives, Krepps also tests to see whether BIA high-skill labor adds more to the timber price than tribal high-skilled labor. Again, his results confirm higher tribal productivity compared to BIA control; a 10 percent increase in tribal high-skilled labor adds 5.9 percent to price, while the same increment of BIA labor adds only 1.4 percent. Krepps concludes that "the findings that high-skilled tribally controlled foresters do a better job of marketing tribal timber than BIA agents provides hard evidence to support anecdotal instances of BIA malfeasance" (1992, p. 197).

Interestingly, the Krepps data also support the finding presented here regarding individual control relative to tribal control. In his estimates of annual harvest relative to AAC, Krepps finds that a larger percentage of allottee ownership increases harvest by "1.34 million bf per year given the AAC and the degree of tribal involvement" (1992, p. 189). These results are consistent with the hypothesis that accountability matters in that individual allottees have more incentive to manage their forests efficiently.[27] It appears that more individual control improves productivity, and this raises questions about Krepps' conclusion that "if the federal trust responsibility has come to signify undercutting Indian forests and selling tribal timber for a fraction of its value, then greater tribal involvement is the only recourse" (p. 200); more individual control would further increase forest productivity as measured by Krepps. Whether tribal or individual, the forestry data suggest "all tribes, regardless of wealth or experience, enjoy a decided motivational advantage over BIA foresters who are paid flat salaries, regardless of how well they manage Indian forests" (pp. 199–200). The bottom line is that accountability is a key to productivity, and accountability is difficult to obtain under the trusteeship of a large federal bureaucracy.

Conclusion

Economic development on Indian reservations is related to many variables, not the least of which are land tenure constraints. Because of the trust status of Indian resources, the costs of organizing inputs for agricultural production are higher than with fee simple tenure. Collective management need not reduce productivity if tribal governance structures can prevent "those who exercise the legitimate powers of government from using that power to transfer wealth" (Cornell & Kalt, 1992b, p. 25). The data show that the value of agricultural output on individual lands is significantly lower than on fee simple lands and that tribal trust lands do even worse, controlling for other variables that might influence output. Because trust constraints also govern other Indian resources such as forests, coal, oil, and minerals, their development also is likely to be limited compared with similar privately owned resources. Knowing that the costs associated with trust arrangements reduce the value of output does not necessarily imply that these constraints should be lifted or that fee simple ownership is preferable. It does, however, give some idea of the cost of constraining the ability of Indians to make their own decisions about resource use.

Notes

1. This chapter is partly extracted from Anderson and Lueck (1992a) and Anderson and Lueck (1992b).

2. For a discussion of expenditures on the various efforts to augment these stocks, see U.S. Department of the Interior (1986).

3. See Carlson (1981, 1992) for a full discussion of this issue.

4. For a further discussion of the tradeoffs associated with private versus common ownership of land, see Lueck (1993).

5. For a discussion of the problems of assigning property rights under homesteading rules, see Anderson and Hill (1983).

6. Carlson (1981) noted that the trust lands "declined from 104.3 million acres in 1890 to 52.7 million acres in 1933" (p. 158).

7. These percentages were calculated from U.S. Department of the Interior, Bureau of Indian Affairs (1987) data that showed 54,339,757 acres of Indian Land; 42,104,294 acres of tribally owned trust land; 10,621,712 acres of individually owned trust land; and 1,191,562 acres of government land. An additional 422,189 acres were unclassified as to ownership status.

8. There were many allotments before the Dawes Act, but they were the result of legislation aimed at particular reservations or tribes. Some of these early allotments gave the individual Indians fee title to their allotments. The Dawes Act set up a general policy of allotment for nearly all reservations. See National Congress of American Indians (1968) and Washburn (1971).

9. The term *essentially* is used because the tribes do have limited regulatory power within the reservation even for fee lands. Such authority has become more of an issue in recent years as tribes have claimed additional land and use rights. Twenty years ago, bureau and tribal concern was solely with trust lands; reservation boundaries were of little concern. Granting recent tribal claims to territorial rights for such use as fishing and hunting, however, has increased the interest of tribes in control of land for certain uses extending to the reservation border and sometimes beyond.

10. Technically, title can be held by the individuals, in which case it is referred to as *restricted fee,* or title can be held by the U.S. government, in which case it is referred to as *trust allotted.* For purposes here, the term *individual trust* is used to refer to both categories, which, for all practical purposes, have the same trust constraints.

11. For a more complete discussion of heirship, see Williams (1970–1971). Because fee simple lands are not subject to these heirship rules and because tribal trust lands cannot be willed, heirship problems are not present with these two tenures.

12. There are minor exceptions to this in cases where tribes have purchased fee simple land, especially outside the reservation. In general, however, when the tribe purchases fee simple land, the land is placed into trust status.

13. Indeed, the capital problem seems serious. Conversations with Bureau of Indian Affairs officials, Indians, and business owners indicate that local banks tend to *completely* avoid Indian farmers with trust lands because their land cannot be used to cover defaults on loans.

14. For a discussion of regulations regarding leasing under heirship, see 25 CFR Ch. 1 (4-1-89 Edition) 162.

15. Note that the analysis uses gross value. The net rental value of land will also be reduced, but available data do not allow a test of this hypothesis.

16. For a detailed discussion of the relationship between output and tenure, see Anderson and Lueck (1992b).

17. In cases where reservations cross county lines, a weighted average of county data was used where the weights were the proportion of the reservation in each county.

18. These data were taken from Part 6 and Part 2, respectively, of *Natural Resources Information System* (U.S. Department of the Interior, Bureau of Indian Affairs, 1987) for each reservation. The reason for using acres with agricultural potential rather than the actual acres in production is that some acres are idle or "underemployed" because of trust constraints. If Indians are able to overcome the higher costs inherent in trust constraints, output per acre should be similar to fee simple land. Using potential acres recognizes that trust constraints can keep land underemployed or out of production.

19. Given the mean of 0.54 and the standard deviation of 0.495, the hypothesis that trust land and private land are equally productive can be rejected at the 99 percent confidence level.

20. Total Indian output was taken from Part 6 of *Natural Resources Information System* (U.S. Department of the Interior, Bureau of Indian Affairs, 1987). The value of fee simple output was computed by multiplying the value of fee simple output per acre

(reported in Table 6.2) times fee simple acres (reported in Table 6.1).

21. Note that this construction biases the results against the hypothesis because it assumes that all fee simple land on reservations is producing cultivated crops. To the extent that some of this land would be in lower valued production per acre, such as livestock, the value of actual reservation output would be lower and the actual ratio smaller.

22. For a complete discussion of the other variables used in the statistical analysis, see Anderson and Lueck (1992b, pp. 446–447). One variable of particular importance was whether the land was being used by Indians or non-Indians. If Indian farmers have fewer farming skills than their non-Indian counterparts and represent a higher proportion of the reservation farmers, the value of total output from all reservation land will decline relative to the value of output from fee simple land regardless of tenure. The statistical results suggest that this was not a very important variable for explaining differences in productivity.

23. For details of this regression analysis, see Anderson and Lueck (1992b, pp. 446–448.)

24. It could be argued that the Wind River and Standing Rock Reservations are outliers and therefore should be dropped from the sample. Dropping them lowers the mean ratio to 0.88, still a surprising result given that most believe that Indians got the worst land.

25. For a detailed discussion of the settlements, see Smith (1992).

26. Annual allowable cut is a measure of the annual harvest rate that can be sustained from a forest given biological constraints such as tree growth rate, current and expected future timber prices, and interest rates. For further discussion, see Krepps (1992, p. 184).

27. Krepps attributes this higher rate of harvest to the possibility that "individuals' rates of time preference do not include the full consideration of descendants that may characterize tribal decision makers" (1992, p. 186). Unfortunately, his data do not allow a separation of these two hypotheses.

CHAPTER 7

Constitutions and Culture

The allotment era ended with the Indian Reorganization Act (IRA) of 1934, another law supported by reformers bent on imposing the right institutional framework on Indians. Led by Commissioner of Indian Affairs John Collier, these reformers believed they were offering "a model of community that all Americans might in some ways follow" (U.S. Department of Interior, 1986, p. 72). Collier would not heed warnings from anthropologists regarding the likely success of the proposed IRA, "because he wanted the Indians to offer an alternate way of living for individualistic-oriented white America" (Philip, 1977, p. 159). Instead of molding Indians into ideal citizens via private ownership as tried under the Dawes Act, the IRA focused on communal organization centered around tribal governments formulated under constitutions and charters to be ratified through a democratic process. In the world of never ending policy reforms, the IRA set Indians on a new tack toward centralized tribal government.

The New Deal Indian policy encompassed in the IRA might have taken Indians a long way toward self-determination, but the institutional changes that actually occurred further ensconced federal bureaucracies as trustees of their Indian wards.

Rather than allowing Indians to adapt their institutions in ways consistent with their cultural heritage, the New Dealers tried to make tribal governments the model for collective action. Unfortunately, "Collier's insistence that all Indians develop a closely knit communal existence similar to the New Mexico Pueblos proved impractical" (Philip, 1977, p. 165) for all but a few tribes. But Collier's efforts did institutionalize some tribal governments that, in some cases, are hardly more accountable than their federal trustees. Out of this reform, the tribe and its relationship with the federal government became the focus of attention with little consideration given sub-groups or individuals. At the same time, Collier's administration did little to reduce the influence of the Washington bureaucracy on Indians but instead demonstrated that the BIA could flex its muscle in ways that left Congress out of the policy picture (see Deloria, 1985, pp. 249–250).

In this chapter, I survey the relationship among individual Indians, their tribal governments, and the federal government after the Indian Reorganization Act of 1934. The IRA was a missed opportunity because it failed to blend the necessary constitutional limits on tribal government with the heritage of each tribe. When Collier's efforts at collective reform failed to receive support from the tribes, post-World War II policy focused on termination of reservations and integration of Indians into the larger society. For those who integrated, opportunities expanded and incomes rose, but they generally had to leave their reservations and their culture to enjoy these fruits. For those who remained on the reservations, the only hope for escaping poverty hung on federal programs. Instead of reducing Indian dependence on the federal government and encouraging self-determination, modern policies have diversified Indian programs into a multitude of federal agencies and locked Indians into a political world where their wealth depends on their ability to receive transfer payments from the federal government.

A Missed Opportunity

Early New Deal reforms included legislation introduced by Representatives Edgar Howard of Nebraska and Burton K.

Wheeler of Montana that would end allotment and allow Indians to discard the "shallow and unsophisticated individualism" (John Collier, cited in Philip, 1977, p. 161) that Commissioner Collier believed accompanied private control of natural and human resources. Just as the Lake Mohonk Friends of the Indian led late nineteenth-century Indian reform on the ground that allotment would promote the Jeffersonian ideal among landed Indians, a variety of organizations ranging from the American Indian Defense Association to the American Civil Liberties Union led the crusade for communal reform under the IRA. Inspired by a private investigation of the BIA by Lewis Meriam under the auspices of the Institute for Government Research, John Collier held a conference at the Cosmos Club in Washington, D.C., on January 7, 1934, to consider the recommendations of the Meriam report titled *The Problem of Indian Administration*. Delegates to the conference unanimously concluded that they "wanted to repeal the land allotment law, consolidate Indian heirship and trust lands for agricultural purposes, promote tribal ownership of grazing and forest lands, and acquire additional land for landless Indians" (Philip, 1977, pp. 135–136). This support inspired Collier to press forward with his reforms.

Even before the IRA was introduced to Congress by Representatives Wheeler and Howard, Collier ran his proposals up the flag pole only to have a volley of shots fired by various Indian tribes. His plan for Indian self-government called on Indians to adopt constitutions or charters that would give them a governing structure capable of replacing the Indian Bureau and proposed land reform on reservations that would establish tribal, as opposed to individual, control.

> Collier must have been dismayed by the negative response from many Indian tribes and their superintendents. Opposition proved strong on reservations where land allotment had broken down tribal life. Americanized Indians, who had become assimilated, were especially hostile to his circular. They objected to relinquishing individual allotments for community ownership and feared that the creation of self-governing communities would restore outdated traditions.

Many superintendents also opposed the measure because it might eliminate their jobs. (Philip, 1977, p. 138)

Two questions immediately arise from this opposition. The first is just how bad was the allotment? Today stories abound about how disastrous allotment was for Indians. Senator Dawes himself was concerned with "the greed and hunger and thirst of the white man for the Indian's land" (cited in Prucha, 1984, p. 670).

Year by year, in fact, the process of allotment was stepped up, and the surplus lands were rapidly transferred to the whites. The Indians held 155,632,312 acres in 1881; by 1890 they had 104,314,349, and by 1900 only 77,865,373, of which 5,409,530 had been allotted. So successful did the process seem that the reformers looked forward to the day when government supervision over the Indians would disappear entirely and the Indians would all be absorbed into American society. (Prucha, 1984, p. 671)

Though the transfer of Indian lands to whites is taken as prima facie evidence of the failure of privatization, McChesney notes that the failure may have been "caused by a lack of private ownership, especially the fact that allottees had only equitable ownership of their lands. As legal owner, the government as trustee maintained substantial rights for twenty-five years after allotment. Allotment did not entail full privatization" (1992, p. 110).

The fact that opposition to Collier's reforms was strongest in areas where allotment had progressed the most suggests that some Indians had adjusted quite well to allotment. Throughout Indian Country, tribes and individuals responded like the Arapaho tribe on the Wind River Reservation in Wyoming: "They called the idea of community government foreign to the Plains Indians and opposed communal ownership of property as unsuited to their tribe" (Philip, 1977, p. 139). Though we may never have accurate measures of the impact of allotment,[1] the opposition from Indian allottees to Colliers communal land reform suggests that at least those allottees saw merit in private ownership.

The second question is what role did the bureaucracy play in the New Deal reform? As discussed in Chapter 5, McChesney's evidence suggests that bureaucrats are at least survivors if not budget maximizers. Had allotment continued, the Bureau of Indian Affairs might have worked itself out of a job, and indeed the number of employees of the BIA actually declined from 6000 to 5000 between 1911 and 1933. But the guarantee of BIA trusteeship and expanded managerial and educational functions recommended in the Meriam report in 1928 virtually guaranteed expansion. Deloria notes that "the most important change in this period was not the General Allotment Act . . . but the amendments to the Allotment Act, which shifted the theoretical base of allotment from an educative process whereby Indians could learn how to manage private property to an administrative problem in which the federal government was assumed to be the supervisor of how Indian property was to be used" (1985, p. 247). Not surprisingly, this expanded the administrative powers of the BIA, and the number of employees increased to 12,000 between 1933 and 1934 (see Taylor, 1984, p. 35).

Despite opposition to his reform proposals, Collier was undaunted in his efforts and succeeded in having President Roosevelt sign the IRA into law on June 18, 1934. In addition to ending allotment, the act authorized Congress to spend $250,000 annually for the purpose of formalizing governmental entities on reservations and an additional $2 million annually for land acquisition. Tribal councils were to adopt constitutions and by-laws that would allow the councils to control leasing or sale of land, borrow money, negotiate with the federal and state governments, and generally conduct business for the tribe.

Though he succeeded in getting Congress to pass and the president to sign the IRA, "Collier's zeal for reestablishing communal life" (Philip, 1977, p. 162) could only be realized on those reservations where a majority of the adult Indians voted in favor of the IRA. Again, tribal opposition became evident. To increase the likelihood that the vote was favorable, the Department of the Interior solicitor's office ruled that abstentions— votes not cast—would count as favorable, and in some cases federal grants and loans were tied to a favorable vote. These schemes notwithstanding, 181 tribes with a population of

129,750 approved the act, while 77 tribes totaling 86,365 members repudiated it (Deloria & Lytle, 1984, p. 172). In general, the IRA faced so much opposition because Collier failed to heed the warnings of anthropologists and Indians alike who stated that communal organization based on democratic rules would be inimical to many tribes.

> These romantic ideas . . . faced opposition from the Indians who favored assimilation, as well as from congressmen, missionaries, bureau personnel, and the Indian Rights Association. Their concept of Indian progress originated from a different reform tradition which stressed the desirability of the melting pot concept. (Philip, 1977, p. 160)

Collier's reforms began with the premise that *all* Indians had a heritage of communal organization and that formal constitutions would solve the problems inherent in governmental structures. In fact, he was wrong on both counts. Among the Plains Indians there was little tradition of centralized control. Buffalo hunts and war parties required careful organization and were coordinated by chiefs, but everyday life on the Plains was quite autonomous. Hence, it is not surprising that the Sioux, Arapaho, Assiniboine, and Blackfeet objected to Collier's plan. Even for those with a history of communal organization, the experience of two generations with assimilation made returning to old ways difficult. In cases like the Jicarilla and Mescalero Apaches, which were closely knit tribes, however, Collier's ideas did find support and success (Philip, 1977).

The main problem with the IRA approach was that it tried to use the same communal recipe for all tribes when it should have been clear that all Indian tribes are not one homogeneous cultural unit. In particular, Collier's insistence on a communal existence manifested itself in many of the constitutions put before the tribes.

> The preambles implied a restoration of tribal sovereignty and possible segregation from white society. Several constitutions established separate Indian courts, and gave tribal councils power to . . . regulate the inheritance of property other than allotted lands.

> Many Indians who had kept their allotments disliked
> the constitutions because they allowed landless Indi-
> ans to have a preference in the assignment of tribal
> real estate. (Philip, 1977, p. 165)

For some tribes the allotment path to privatization may have
been inimical to tradition, but once the die was cast those
individuals who began working their land found it difficult to
give up control to the collective. For other tribes, the communal
organization pushed by the Collier reformers had no basis in
individualistic traditions.

Instead of allowing Indians to adopt constitutions consistent with their heritage, Collier used the IRA to mold and
reform all Indians in his communal image. Collier brought
anthropological experts to Washington to promote his ideas.
The irrelevancy of his approach is highlighted by the fact that
he used presentations on the communal successes among the
Irish and among consumer movements in the United States to
support his program for reform. Even the bureau's chief anthropologist, Scudder Mekeel, argued that there was "a conceptual
flaw in the act; it tried to impose rigid white political and
economic concepts in a situation which called for flexibility. . . .
Although Indian constitutions varied, they were patterned
after the United States Constitution rather than tribal custom"
(Philip, 1977, p. 164). Moreover, under the tribal constitutions,
the powers of elected leaders corresponded to Anglo-American
governmental institutions and derived from democratic elections. "To many Indian people, especially those who have
knowledge of their traditional tribal value systems, democratic
elections more often than not create artificial elites who then
rule more or less in an arbitrary manner. . . . According to many
traditional value systems, however, authority is vested in individuals" on the basis of whether they have "excelled in certain
skills, practiced generosity, displayed great courage, have
knowledge of ceremonial functions, possess spiritual powers, or
who have strong analytical abilities or wisdom" (Holm, 1985,
pp. 135–136). It was because the IRA did not integrate a
constitutional framework consistent with traditional "rules of
the game" for the various tribes that the IRA was a missed
opportunity that led to another failed Indian policy.

The Bureaucratic Yoyo

With a post-World War II society fixed on allowing everyone the opportunity to join the middle class, federal policy turned toward integrating Indians into the white man's culture. Yet another report was issued by the Senate Committee on Indian Affairs in 1943. This report was critical of the IRA efforts "to keep the Indian an Indian" and to "recapture his ancient, worn-out cultures" when non-Indians were making no effort "to recapture our glamorous pioneer culture." The committee believed that existing policies were "segregating the Indian from the general citizenry" and "condemning the Indian to perpetual wardship" (U.S. Senate, 1943, p. 18). The Senate committee questioned "whether the Indian New Deal was moving the Indians toward real self-sufficiency, which would mean the end of federal guardianship and absorption into the mass of the nation's citizenry, or whether the bureau was building up and perpetuating itself, continuing its guardianship as the Indians returned to the tribalism and their old ways" (Prucha, 1984, p. 335). In 1944 the House concurred with its own report, stating that the goal of Indian policy should be to help the Indian "take his place in the white man's community on the white man's level and with the white man's opportunity and security status" (U.S. House of Representatives, 1944, p. 2).

To reverse the emphasis on the tribe, federal policy shifted toward termination of federal jurisdiction over Indians. The rhetoric of termination focused on integrating Indians into the rest of society, with the objectives of the BIA to promote "(1) a standard of living for Indians comparable with that enjoyed by other segments of the population, and (2) the step-by-step transfer of Bureau functions to the Indians themselves or to the appropriate agencies of local, state or federal government" (Commissioner of Indian Affairs, 1951, p. 353). Included in the termination policies was an effort to relocate Indians from their reservations to urban areas where it was felt they could integrate better into non-Indian society. In 1953 Congress passed House and Senate Concurrent Resolution 108, calling for termination of Indian reservations, and between 1954 and 1962, 12 termination acts were passed.

Because the policy of termination meant the loss of bureaucratic and tribal power and budget, it is not surprising that by the 1960s policy was shifting back toward a heavy reliance on tribal government and the reservation as the main determinants of Indian life. The states, which were receiving federal funds to administer Indian affairs under the 12 termination acts, reversed their position and began returning funds and authority to the federal government (see Taylor, 1984, p. 26).

With the end of termination efforts came renewed emphasis on economic, social, and government development on reservations accompanied by additional federal spending. Lyndon Johnson's War on Poverty

> resulted in a variety of new Federal programs which, cumulatively, sharply increased the level of Federal expenditures on Indians. Moreover, the administration of new Federal Indian programs was different; instead of the BIA, the programs were administered by other agencies, many of them largely responsible to a nonIndian constituency. . . . The war on poverty then led to a major erosion in the role of the BIA in Indian Affairs. By 1984, the BIA was responsible for only 33 percent of total Federal expenditures on Indians. Fifty years earlier, the corresponding figure would have been close to 100 percent. (U.S. Department of Interior, 1986, p. 73)

Table 7.1 shows how the responsibility for funding Indian programs shifted between 1973 and 1985. During this short period, the Department of Interior's share declined by more than 20 percent.

Under Presidents Johnson and Nixon yet another new policy, self-determination, began to take shape, although it has come to little. Both presidents had a similar agenda:

> a rejection of the termination policy; the need for Indian involvement; develop Indian leadership; expand credit; improve schools and Indian participation in their operation; and emphasize the transfer of control and responsibility from the federal government to Indian communities rather than to state or

local government, but with continued federal responsibility for funding, services, and technical assistance. (Taylor, 1984, p. 26).

It is the latter objectives that have thwarted progress toward self-determination. With the government responsible for "funding, services, and technical assistance," the corresponding agencies are not likely to give up the strings of control. To do so could spell political suicide. Moreover, the broadened bureaucratic base resulting from diversification of funding gave more agencies a stake in perpetuating wardship. The same survival characteristics that led the BIA to switch its position on allotment prompted the many agencies with budgetary interests to lobby for additional funding and control.

Self-determination as defined under Public Law 93-638, the Indian Self-Determination and Educational Assistance Act of 1975, did not really mean that Indians would be free of the puppet strings of federal bureaucracies. It specified that it was

TABLE 7.1 Percent of Total Federal Indian Expenditures by Department or Agency

Agency or department	1973	1981	1985
Agriculture	2.4	1.8	2.5
Commerce	2.9	0.9	0.4
Education	—	12.2	11.0
Energy	—	—	neg
HHS	37.3	26.6	32.4
HUD	3.2	11.7	10.8
Interior	46.4	40.8	36.5
Labor	4.4	5.7	2.5
Transportation	—	—	3.4
Treasury	—	0.4	0.4
EPA	—	—	neg
SBA	1.8	—	0.1

Note: neg = negligible

Source: U.S. Department of the Interior (1986, p. 89).

"the obligation of the United States to respond to the strong expressions of the Indian people for self-determination by assuming maximum Indian participation in the direction of . . . Federal services to the needs and desires of those communities" (93rd Congress, S. 1017, January 4, 1975 [25 U.S.C. §450]: 1). This interpretation of self-determination meant that Indians would be given more say in federal programs, but it did not really free them from the bonds of wardship. Rather than change the rules of the game under which tribal governments operate, it encouraged tribal leaders to invest in obtaining political clout by being the ones to control federal benefits. However, because the money was still channeled through federal agencies, it is not surprising that "the act quickly became entangled with exceptions as career bureaucrats resisted the policy of turning large areas of responsibility over to the Indians" (Deloria, 1985, p. 253).

At the tribal level, the increased possibility of federal funds and the greater diversity of agencies controlling those funds meant that "tribal governments generally had to learn how to operate in a much broader political and economic environment than the traditional relationship with BIA" (U.S. Department of the Interior, 1986, p. 73). The Interior Department Task Force concluded that this experience "played a critical role in the significant improvements in the administrative skills and general capabilities of many tribal governments in the 1960s and 1970s" (p. 74). But it is unclear whether administrative skills associated with obtaining governmental transfers are transferable to productive activities on reservations. Initially, the War on Poverty focused on investment in capital, manpower training, and technical assistance that would provide long-term economic development, but that soon changed to more direct expenditures for health care, roads, housing, and other infrastructure. Although Indians certainly gained directly from these goods and services and indirectly from employment associated with the government programs, "Indians have been left perhaps even more dependent than before on the Federal Government for income, employment and general provision for their economic welfare. Indians are subject to swings in the political fortunes of the Federal programs on which they now depend" (p. 90). Rather than moving in the direction of greater self-determination, "the level of discretion available to tribal governments in spending Federal funds has declined" (p. 90). Indeed, one-fifth of all federal expenditures pays for bureaucratic overhead, and one-third of the BIA budget goes to its regulatory and supervisory functions regarding the government's trust responsibility (see Barsh & Diaz-Knauf, 1984). Thus, the administrative skills acquired by the tribes have not been those that would promote sustainable economic development but rather have been those that would guarantee a larger piece of the federal pie, even while that pie was decreasing. "That some tribal officials regarded this financial support as fulfilling previous treaty commitments is all the more tragic because this interpretation of federal assistance gave an artificial boost to the emerging doctrine of tribal sovereignty that distorted the Indian vision of political and economic reality" (Deloria, 1985, p. 251).

Politics As Usual in Tribal Government

An excellent case study in *Tribal Government Today* (Lopach, Brown, & Clow, 1990) considers the politics of Montana Indian reservations and illustrates the legacy of the IRA. Each of the seven Montana reservations has a slightly different form of government, and some show much more economic progress than others. Nonetheless, the institutional environment on the reservations is generally not one that links the authority given to tribal politicians and federal bureaucrats with a responsibility to the tribe.

The Crow tribe is perhaps the quintessential example of the democratic process run amok. Under the Crow constitution, the tribal council, which is the decision-making body for the tribe, is composed of the entire adult membership of the tribe and has wide discretion in its control of decisions affecting the tribe. Lopach, Brown, and Clow argue that "the Crows' conduct of their general council meeting makes it a perfect vehicle for perpetuating a patronage system" because "that kind of politics needs a reliable method of rewarding friends and punishing enemies" (1990, p. 65). In this system, federal funds are misused, employment worksheets are falsified, and access to tribal resources such as grazing is a political plum. According to one tribal member, "like grass-hoppers clans jump back and forth between factions" (p. 65) to garner political rewards. Hence, tribal politics "is about who controls government and, therefore, who controls jobs and the dispensation of benefits" (p. 66).

This pure democratic form of government, which allocates power on the basis of votes, runs counter to the traditional Crow culture that emphasized the individual. Traditional Crow hierarchy gave power only on a limited basis to hunt chiefs and to war chiefs so that "the people hardly felt the weight of authority" (Lowie, 1935, p. 6). The exception that plays into the modern patronage system was the power that could be garnered by a family or clan. Based on the size and status of a clan, some individuals could gain social status and power, and "with the aid of his relatives, this exception to the Crow ideal of autonomy could use the absence of formal checks to 'easily dominate a band of a few hundred souls'" (Lopach, Brown, & Clow, 1990, p. 59). With this exception firmly ensconced in the Crows' constitutional democracy adopted under the IRA, individual autonomy has been supplanted by a political tyranny with few checks and balances. Not surprisingly, despite a vast wealth of grazing land, coal, timber, water, and wildlife, the Crow tribe is near the bottom of the economic heap. Nearly 75 percent of the workforce is unemployed. Most of those who are employed hold government jobs, and half the population receives some form of federal assistance. The lack of congruence between traditional individual freedom and the political process combined with the ability of political leaders to manipulate tribal resources for their and their supporters' benefit locks the Crow tribe into an institutional system conducive to political transfers but not to productivity.

At the other end of the spectrum in Montana is the Flathead Reservation, made up of a confederation of the Salish and Kootenai people. Like so many others, the Flathead tribes, which were the first to adopt a constitution under the IRA in 1936, adopted a structure that reflected the Anglo-American conception of government. Although the constitution did not reflect their traditional political structures that included "a council of headmen, a system of leadership including a head chief and lesser chiefs, and a pronounced ethic of individual autonomy" (Lopach, Brown, & Clow, 1990, p. 157), the tribes were open to new governing ideas and strived to adapt. Even before the term *self-determination* had found its way into political rhetoric, the Flathead tribes were flexing their muscle. By 1944 the tribal council requested that the Office of Indian Affairs leave the reservation and that they be given full control of tribal resources. Of course, this early quest for self-determination met resistance from the bureaucracy and the formal request to try tribal administration was rejected. Instead of self-rule, the ensuing 40 years brought dominance by the agency superintendent and the BIA.

Their efforts to remove federal supervision, however, "made the Flathead reservation a candidate for the eventual complete withdrawal of federal regulation" (Lopach, Brown, & Clow, 1990, p. 159). Dissatisfied with the bureau's heavy-handed trusteeship role and with the political favoritism that were coming to dominate tribal politics, in the 1970s the tribal council began moving to unshackle itself from the BIA. The general view of the BIA was one of a "smug bureaucracy operating without comment, access, or accountability. A common judgement is that the Bureau makes no contribution at all to the welfare of the tribes" (Lopach, Brown, & Clow, 1990, p. 162). The tribal government began asserting itself by implementing structural reforms that bypassed the BIA, streamlining the tribal committees, and establishing a chain of command that created accountability for tribal leaders.

Though the reforms did not necessarily reflect the traditional political organization for the tribes, they did represent a blend of traditional and borrowed rules that encourage productivity. The Flathead reservation "operates under a constitutional parliamentary system and an effectively separate (i.e., professional and legislatively protected) judiciary. This provides a system of formal separation of powers and of 'checks and balances' of the type often associated with western democracies" (Cornell & Kalt, 1992a, p. 236). This at least partly explains why the Salish and Kootenai Confederated Tribes enjoy one of the lower reservation unemployment rates (though it is still high relative to off-reservation standards) and higher growth rates among Indian reservations.

Between these two extremes are a variety of tribal governments that have had more or less success at providing an institutional environment conducive to economic development. Lopach, Brown, and Clow (1990) emphasize four measures of reservation progress: good leadership, including stability; effective political structure, including the separation of powers and formal procedures; adequate revenue combined with fiscal restraint; and reservation unity, meaning shared values, pride and homogeneity, "whether based upon common roots or practical experience" (p. 187). Assessed against these four criteria, they conclude that "the Montana reservations have a considerable range. Flathead, Fort Peck, Northern Cheyenne, and the Blackfeet are grouped toward the top, and Crow, Fort Belknap, and Rocky Boys' have the greatest distance to travel" (p. 187). To be sure, none of these reservations can claim to have solved the economic growth puzzle, since all have unemployment rates ranging from a low of 20 percent (Flathead) to a high of 72 percent (Rocky Boys). Nonetheless, this survey of Montana reservations confirms that any economic progress will be elusive if tribes are unable to develop political environments that foster stability for investment in both physical and human capital.

The Institutional Crucible

It is becoming increasingly clear to Indian scholars that reservation development is less a function of resource endowments, physical or human, though these do make some difference, and more a function of the institutional environment. Certainly, a society with no resource endowment or no knowledge of how to use its endowment would have little possibility for survival. However, if the endowment is used in the most efficient manner, the society can maximize its potential output.

Reservations vary in their endowments and in their ability to utilize them, but these differences generally do not explain economic development. The Crow tribe, for example, is one of the largest owners of coal reserves in the world and had total assets estimated at $26,820,779,087 ($3,283,000 per capita) in 1988. Yet these assets earn only about $3 million annually for an appalling rate of return of 0.01 percent per annum (Cornell & Kalt, 1992a, p. 224). Moreover, the Crow have high levels of education; 52 percent of the adult population has graduated from high school (Cornell & Kalt, 1991, p. 1). Between 1977 and 1989, the percentage of Crows earning incomes above the BIA minimum declined by 12 percent. Alternatively, the Blackfeet reservation is almost 40 percent smaller, has no coal reserves, has some oil and gas, and abundant grass and timber. Unemployment on the Blackfeet reservation was 45 percent in 1989, and the percentage of Blackfeet adults earning above the BIA minimum rose by 4 percent between 1977 and 1989. There are 24,000 Indian owned cattle compare to 31,000 non-Indian owned cattle grazing on the reservation. In 1981, oil and gas royalties amounted to over $3 million out of a total tribal income of $4,573,807 (Lopach, Brown, & Clow, 1990, p. 45). The bottom line is that the Blackfeet are doing better than the Crows despite the fact that they have fewer resources.

Obviously, the efficiency with which a tribe's resource endowment is used determines economic success,[2] and this in turn depends on the institutional environment. The crucial question is: What incentives do individuals in both the private and political sectors have to improve the efficiency of resource allocation? Historically Indian culture has demonstrated an ability to survive and even develop by making the most of its resource endowments. But bureaucratic constraints have left their negative mark on the ability of individuals and tribes to utilize trust resources efficiently. Regardless of resource endowments and the knowledge of how to use them, the rules of the game ultimately determine whether societies prosper or decline. If these rules channel resources toward productive activities, foster investments that have long-run returns, and encourage gains from trade, prosperity is more likely. If they redistribute wealth in a zero-sum game or create uncertainty about the future instead, poverty is more likely.

How well the rules of the game work to expand opportunities depends on whether political agents are held accountable to their citizens. An obvious example of the lack of accountability is corruption. If a tribal leader can pocket the returns from exploiting tribal resources for his or her own use, there is little to guarantee that tribal members will benefit. As evidenced by races for congressional seats at the national level or seats on the council at the tribal level, wherever there is political power, there will be a scramble to obtain the power and wealth of leadership.

Therefore, the fundamental problem of political economy is how to endow the collectivity known as government with enough power to establish and enforce rules that can expand the size of the economic pie without that power being used to garner returns for those with the power. To the extent that political power can be used to redistribute wealth as opposed to create it, individuals will compete to capture that power through what economists call rent seeking. Campaign contributions will be made and expended, lobbying will dominate the decision-making process, and political favors will be returned for support. As resources are consumed in the rent-seeking competition, the size of the economic pie shrinks. Short-term decisions that enhance the wealth and power of those in control are substituted for long-term true economic development.[3]

In private contracts, we ultimately rely on a third party impartial enforcer, usually government provided courts,[4] to arbitrate disputes and guarantee performance. But with government itself the enforcer of rules, there is no impartial third party enforcer to which citizens can turn for recourse. For example, it is clear that rules governing behavior at stop signs make for orderly passage at busy intersections. To enforce those rules, we have police. But what stops the police from handing out special rights to passage to certain individuals or stops them from disobeying the rules themselves? The power of enforcement any society grants its government can be used to redistribute the wealth in favor of those with power. Therefore, to prevent usurpation of that power, societies attempt to establish higher order rules or constitutional limits to constrain the powers of government. We give the police the power to enforce rules at intersections, but we build in checks to discourage the use of that power for personal gain by our political or bureaucratic agents.

The constitutions adopted under the Indian Reorganization Act were a step in the right direction to the extent that they addressed this fundamental problem of political economy. But effective constitutions must be contracts that reflect agreements among the population governed, and the IRA constitutions were not necessarily like this. They did establish procedures for selecting and removing tribal councils, separating executive, legislative, and judicial powers, and instituting democratic procedures, all of which can curtail rent seeking. But the results of the IRA experiment with constitutional constraints have been mixed. The corruption that characterized politics on the Navajo reservation under Peter McDonald and the political maneuvering within the Crow tribal council to capture returns for those with short-term control illustrate cases where the limits have been ineffective. In contrast, the more successful political structure on the Flathead reservation shows that some of the problems of rent seeking can be avoided.

One reason that the IRA experiment with constitutional limits has not been a total success is that the adopted rules often have little connection with the tribe's institutional heritage. The constitutions presented to the tribes by the BIA were patterned after the U.S. Constitution with its democratic principles. But democracy had little place in the traditional cultures of most tribes. The collective structure molded in Collier's image of what Indians were supposed to be also ran into conflict with the rugged individualism so prevalent among the Plains tribes. What should be obvious is that the rules of the game adopted without the benefit of evolution and without consideration for the cultural environment in which the rules must operate are unlikely to be sufficient to promote prosperity. The written, formal rules adopted in the IRA constitutions were often at odds with the unwritten, informal, implicit rules that evolved through tradition. This problem is exacerbated on reservations such as Fort Peck where different tribal cultures have been forced to blend. The political cultures of the Assiniboine and Sioux were quite different. "The Assiniboine governed themselves through many groups, each subject to laws which were spotty in coverage and carried little authority. The Sioux also were divided into bands, but government within each was characterized by strict rule and rigorous enforcement" (Lopach, Brown & Clow, 1990, p. 102). Little wonder that there is factionalism and political conflict "based upon dissimilar heritage, memberships, and ideology" (p. 102). The importance of tradition is illustrated with private property in the U.S. Constitution, which guarantees a person's right to property and allows the powers of government to be used to enforce those rights. But this may be a minor part of the actual protection of property rights we enjoy. The Anglo-American tradition of respect for private property and of not allowing government to take property rights without due process and just compensation may do more to protect property rights than laws and locks. Indeed, without that tradition of respect, it is questionable whether property rights can be enforced. More generally, without a link to cultural constraints that evolve over time and bind societies with informal rules, it is problematic at best to hope that written constitutions can create the institutional environment necessary for prosperity.

Using data from 67 reservations, Cornell and Kalt (1991) attempt to measure the explicit impact of constitutional limits on economic performance and the importance of this cultural link. As a measure of that performance, they consider the percentage change of Indians on a given reservation earning above the BIA minimum and reservation employment between 1977 and 1989. They hypothesize that an independent judiciary is likely to improve economic performance and that those with a general council form of government with all tribal members voting will weaken performance compared to those with a strong chief executive or a strong legislature with a tribal council of seven to 15 members. Controlling for other variables such as education and employment opportunities off-reservation, Cornell and Kalt find that

> employment under strong-chief-executive government is 4 percent-5 percent higher than under general council government. Employment under strong-legislature government is 10 percent-13 percent higher than under a general council system. There is somewhat weaker support for the proposition that independent judiciaries are positive causal factors in tribal development: the contribution is positive at approximately the 70 percent confidence level. (1991, p. 33)

With respect to the impact of tribal government on reservation income, they find that a "strong-chief-executive government is associated with approximately 2 percent more income growth than general council government. . . . Strong-legislature government is associated with 7 percent-10 percent more growth than general council government," but "the independent judiciary does not provide significant independent explanatory power" (p. 34). The implication of their results is that explicit constitutional limits can have a positive impact on economic performance because they reduce the amount of rent seeking.

Cornell and Kalt are quick to note that before concluding that these data argue for a strong chief executive or a strong legislature form of tribal government the overall cultural environment must be considered. Pairing the constitutional form of tribal government with the traditional pattern of tribal governance is a more difficult statistical task. Nonetheless, the efforts by Cornell and Kalt (1991) and Lopach, Brown, and Clow (1990) support the general conclusion that a successful economy is more likely to result if the formal and informal institutions go hand in hand. The experiment with IRA constitutions gave Indians an opportunity to capture one side of the equation, but the insensitivity to traditional informal institutions made the IRA a missed opportunity. It was this insensitivity that led to the concerns of the BIA's chief anthropologist that the IRA constitutions "were patterned after the United States Constitution rather than tribal custom" (Philip, 1977, p. 164). Looking to the future, it seems clear that reservation prosperity will depend on finding the correct mix of formal and informal, written and unwritten, constitutional and cultural constraints on government. "Through careful and sustained attention to constitutional reform, tribal members could formally reclaim their own governments—enshrining the values of the past and building a strong foundation for the future" (Lopach, Brown, & Clow, 1990, p. 189).

Notes

1. For example, it would be useful to know if those Indians who sold their allotted land to whites invested the proceeds in ways that improved their economic position.

2. The same is true of all societies. Argentina was one of the richest countries in the world in the early twentieth century but has fallen dramatically despite the fact that it still has abundant resources. The former Soviet Union was well endowed with resources but had trouble feeding its people. Hong Kong and Taiwan, on the other hand, have few resources but have managed an economic boom in the post-World War II era.

3. For further general discussion of the role of government in promoting productivity activity versus transfer activity, see Anderson and Hill (1980) and North (1990).

4. For a discussion of the possibilities of private enforcement, see Benson (1989).

CHAPTER 8

Myths, Legends,
and Lessons

Typically, the final chapter of a book dealing with Indian history and policy offers policy prescriptions probably aimed at ensuring self-determination and prosperity, but this chapter will not be so bold. When the project began, I had in mind that it would close with such prescriptions, but scholarship teaches an element of humility by showing just how little we actually know about a subject. Jennifer Roback recalled that when a group of us began thinking about issues in property rights and Indian economies "we had high hopes of discovering a property rights innovation that would help the Indians become richer. In many respects, we began with all the enthusiasm of the 'Friends of the Indian' who initiated the disastrous Dawes Act. I am now much less hopeful that the Indians will learn anything from us. On the other hand, we have learned a great deal from them" (1992, p. 24). I share Roback's pessimism about prescribing property rights solutions and her enthusiasm about what scholars can learn from studying Indian institutions and institutional change.

Instead of concluding with a normative policy prescription for what Indians *should* do, in this chapter I will consider what can be learned from Indian history and policy. This approach is more consistent with the foundations of political economy as a positive social science and with the history of Indian policy that says there already has been too much meddling in the affairs of Indians. This is not to say that definitive lessons cannot be learned from the political economy approach taken in the previous chapters. For example, the theory and evidence show that individual freedom and property rights were commonplace prior to interaction with whites (see Chapters 2 and 3) and that modern bureaucratic trust constraints significantly reduce reservation productivity (see Chapter 6).[1] This political economy approach to Indian issues does not necessarily lead to the conclusion that Indian tribes must adopt strict, rectangularly surveyed property rights to land, but it does say that current incentive structures are generally not consistent with Indian traditions and are not promoting productivity on reservations. Whatever the cultural crucible, decision makers—private or political—must be held accountable for their actions. If one thing rings clear from 200 years of Indian policy and centuries of Indian institutional adaptation, it is that local circumstance associated with specific resource and cultural constraints must be taken into account in policy formulation. In the end, individual Indians familiar with these specific circumstances must undertake self-determination. They must decide how to organize their lives and take responsibility for their decisions. Replacing mythology with careful policy analysis can markedly improve this process.

Lesson 1: The Fittest Institutions Survive

Modern scholars allege that primitive societies lived in harmony with nature by developing ideological constraints on behavior. Answering the question "why did industrial civilizations often 'fail' to create sustainable systems in [semiarid regions] while indigenes 'succeeded?'" Olson says, "Indigenous peoples may have consciously chosen to respect the plant and animal communities in their surroundings and erected their religious and ethical systems on this choice. If societies now living in such regions are to change directions and develop a more parsimonious regime, they will have to do so *consciously*" (1989, pp. 22–23). But the argument that it was conscious "respect" for plants and animals that encouraged conservation and even parsimony misses one of the most important lessons from Indian history—institutions constrained the behavior of people by providing positive rewards for good stewardship and negative consequences for bad.

For Indians at the margin of subsistence, a Darwinian evolution of the rules of the game was required for survival. But even those who were fortunate enough to live in more abundant natural environments had to cope with scarce time and capital constraints and with variations in year-to-year harvests. Hames (1987) contends that Indian conservation was not stimulated by a romantic environmental ethic but was a necessary response to this scarcity. It was rules often embodied in customs and traditions that encouraged productive activity. Rules of the game, more than explicit, conscious respect for nature, allowed survival and even prosperity. These rules were perpetuated through religious and ethical systems that formed the cultural foundation of Indian property rights. Especially in the absence of written rules, it is these systems that guide and constrain behavior and determine how successful the society will be at husbanding stocks of natural, physical, and human capital.

When these rules got the incentives right, Indian tribes did well; when they did not, both resources and prosperity suffered. The tribes of the Southwest had well-specified rights to fields and water that gave clans the incentives to invest in settled agriculture and produce abundant crops for a thriving civilization. Individual members of the Plains hunting tribes owned horses and personal property and improved on their physical assets by selectively breeding horses and developing better hunting equipment. With first claim on the animals they harvested, hunters had an incentive to perfect their skills, killing enough game for themselves and those who helped with the butchering. As horses and hunting skills lowered the price of meat, Indians could conserve on labor in hunting and butchering. The lower individual hunting costs also reduced the economies of scale in hunting and reduced the optimal size of socioeconomic units. The Plains horse culture "was characterized by a strong set of distinctive technological, military, social, ritual, and aesthetic patterns . . . derived from . . .

subsistence adaptations on the margins of the Plains" (Bennett, 1989, p. 58). The adaptation to different hunting techniques, larger tepees, and new social organizations did not represent a lifestyle resulting from a loss of respect for nature but rather reflected a predictable response to lower prices and higher wealth. *Homo economicus* was alive and well in the pre-European Indian culture.

Perhaps the most important modern institutional response to changing resource constraints occurred when Indians were confined to reservations. Without interference from the federal government, reservation Indians had little choice but to adapt to their new boundaries. While they did not avail themselves of the rectangular survey and saddle themselves with inappropriately small, 160-acre plots as did the white government, Indians demonstrated that they could organize themselves to survive and adapt to their new circumstances. Agricultural productivity grew as many tribes returned to their pastoral heritage. If the institutional innovation demonstrated during the early reservation years had been allowed to evolve until the present, it is reasonable to assume that discussions of self-determination would not have to be part of the policy agenda.

The history of Indians teaches that institutions and institutional adaptation, more than environmental ethics, are the key to self-determination. Bennett summarizes the importance of this lesson: "To include environmental values in the activity pattern, it is necessary to make them economically profitable so as to encourage choice of alternative, less abusive uses of the land. This will take some doing—something more than a well-meant conservation program. The problems will remain, and only a fundamental change in the institutions will solve them" (1989, p. 72).

Lesson 2: Effective Institutions Evolve from the Bottom Up

The history of western land policy is replete with examples of problems that arise when institutions are imposed from the top down, and Indian policy is no exception. At the end of the Civil

War, the federal government decided to "give away" the public domain to homesteaders willing to suffer the elements for five years. If it was not bad enough that the scheme encouraged premature settlement by whites (see Anderson & Hill, 1991), homesteading forced people to try to make a living on suboptimal land parcels. Similarly, the General Allotment Act attempted to impose a private property system with small land parcels on reservations. Most Indian policy analysts have judged this program a failure because it "shattered Indian homelands and created a class of 100,000 landless people" (Philip, 1986, p. 16). Private land ownership promoted under allotment has been criticized as inimical to Indian culture.

But the problem with allotment and subsequent policies lies in the top down nature of institutional design and not necessarily privatization itself. Prior to allotment, Indians were figuring out how to organize agricultural production on reservations as indicated by the rapid increases in output. They were adapting, although they were not necessarily doing so with formal private property rights to individual land parcels. When allotment was imposed on the reservations, it made no consideration for traditional management schemes that may have embodied abundant knowledge and experience; it assumed that rectangularly surveyed property rights were the only way to get the incentives right.

Given the Indians' demonstrated ability to adapt, they no doubt could have worked—and many did work—within the formal Anglo-American system. However, they were not given an opportunity to do so but were saddled with bureaucratic restrictions that further constrained their ability to discover and develop new institutions. In fact, as McChesney points out, it was not privatization that made allotment a failure but "government retention of trustee responsibilities" under the Indian Reorganization Act that "only weakened property rights" (1992, p. 116).

When the IRA reversed the allotment process in 1934, Indians were again handed a new layer of bureaucracy. The constitutions they were asked to adopt were little more than copies of the U.S. Constitution mixed with a few references to reservations. In some cases, the constitutional constraints have helped make tribal governments more accountable for their actions, but such cases generally are the exception and certainly did not come about because policy reformers searched for and found the proper blend of tradition and constitutional democracy.

I hope we have all learned along with Roback "to appreciate the value of building societies from the bottom up and the destructiveness of trying to reconstruct societies from the top down" (1992, p. 24). This lesson, however, is not just one for white policy reformers. If Indians are to enjoy self-determination, they must begin their reform from the bottom up and shun additional top down federal programs. Indians can learn from the experiences of other societies and should pick and chose from their successes, but each tribe will have to blend its modern institutions with its specific cultural background and the resource constraints of its reservation.

Lesson 3: Trusteeship Promotes Bureaucracy Not Self-Determination

When Chief Justice John Marshall wrote his famous *Cherokee Nation v. Georgia* opinion (30 U.S. [50 Pet.] 1 [1831]), he set the stage for a tension in American policy that persists today. On the one hand, Marshall referred to Indian tribes as "domestic dependent nations," implying that they had alienated their power to negotiate with foreign nations by virtue of treaties with the federal government but that they retained their internal powers to govern themselves. Hence, these "nations within a nation" retained an element of sovereignty. But on the other hand, Marshall likened the relationship between the United States and the tribes to "that of a ward to his guardian," implying that Indians are in some sense weak or lack full faculties so that a stronger party should watch over them. The two seem at opposite ends of a spectrum with the latter, wardship, dominating Indian policy since the 1880s, especially with respect to natural resources.

In reflecting on the circumstances at the time of the General Allotment Act in 1887, the notion of wardship or trusteeship may seem appropriate for societies with little knowledge of fee simple land ownership and real estate markets. Even though Indians were hammering out institutions for governing land allocation on reservations prior to the General Allotment Act, they were by no means familiar with the Anglo-American legal system, especially as it applied to land. The mythical words of Chief Seattle may be fiction, but they do depict the setting for land transactions between Indians and whites: "The President in Washington sends word that he wishes to buy our land. But how can you buy or sell the sky, the land? The idea is strange to us. If we do not own the presence of the air and the sparkle of the water, how can you buy them?" (cited in Wilson, 1992, p. 1452). Who could deny that granting Indians fee simple ownership rights with this backdrop would create a tremendous bargaining opportunity for land-hungry whites? To protect the disadvantaged Indians, the Dawes Act required that allotments be held in trust by the U.S. government until Indian allottees were deemed "competent." Unfortunately, when allotment ended in 1934 with the Indian Reorganization Act, the relationship of ward to guardian was made permanent.

Political economy helps us understand how this came about and what impacts it has had. As trustee of the vast Indian estate, the Bureau of Indian Affairs retains tremendous power over Indian resource allocation. McChesney (1992) explains how maintaining trusteeship enabled the BIA to expand its budget and power. As White (1993) observes:

> In reducing the Indians to wardship, the federal government had enhanced its own power. Congress could, according to the courts, dictate the fates of hundreds of thousands of people in the American West and control tens of thousands of acres of Indian land. In gaining such powers, the federal government had also built up the means to exercise them. The military had subdued the Indians, and a modern bureaucracy, the Bureau of Indian Affairs, had arisen to administer the reservations and steer the government's wards toward citizenship. (p. 117)

With oversight authority regarding tribal natural resource decisions, the BIA can make or break a tribe. It seems probable that BIA trust authority raises transaction costs and drives a wedge between potential gains from trade associated with tribal assets.

The evidence on reservation agricultural productivity and on timber resources presented in Chapter 6 is consistent with this hypothesis. Limits on alienation, leasing, and bequests make it difficult for tribes and individual Indians to borrow against their property and to organize their property into efficient units of production. The statistical conclusion reached in Chapter 6 is that individual and tribal trust lands are 30 to 40 percent and 80 to 90 percent less productive, respectively, than comparable fee simple lands, suggesting that trusteeship is very costly.

Of course, evidence of lower productivity under trusteeship immediately raises the question of whether the restrictions are worth it. These restrictions may protect Indians against ruthless negotiators who would end up with the long end of the stick and prevent the further diminution of the acres in the Indian estate. Indeed, the suggestion of removing federal trusteeship generally raises cries of opposition from Indians themselves. But the tension introduced by Marshall must be considered. If Indians choose to retain trusteeship over their natural resource assets, they must accept the position of the weaker party dominated by the stronger guardian. As with any ward-guardian relationship, this implies less than sovereignty for the ward and rules out the prospect for real self-determination. Trusteeship also brings an obligation by the federal government to be responsible for its wards and may open the federal trough to Indian rent seekers. Choosing to feed at this trough, as so many special interest groups do, reduces autonomy for both the group and its individual members and expands the authority of the bureaucracy. There is an important lesson here, particularly if the goal is self-determination, the ultimate exercise of sovereignty.

Lesson 4: Sovereignty Begins with the Individual

In the twentieth-century search for sovereignty, Indian nations have tried to specify the relationship between tribal governments and local, state, or federal governments. Battles have raged over whether a tribe can allow gambling that is prohibited by the state within which the reservation lies, whether states can tax natural resources owned by a tribe, and whether local zoning authorities can regulate land use on reservations within their boundaries. As sovereign nations within a sovereign nation, Indian tribes claim that other governmental units have no authority over them because "tribal authority was not created by the Constitution—tribal sovereignty predated the formation of the United States and continued after it" (Wilkinson, 1987, pp. 103–104).

The debate has been over whether any government is by Webster's definition "supreme in authority" and if so, which. As with trusteeship, the ambiguity of sovereignty as it applies to Indian nations can be attributed to John Marshall's opinion in *Cherokee Nation v. Georgia* (30 U.S. [50 Pet.] 1 [1831]) and his opinion in *Worcester v. Georgia* (31 U.S. [6 Pet.] 515 [1832]). In the former, Marshall wanted it clear that the federal government ultimately would deal with sovereign nations outside the United States and that the United States was the guardian over Indians. Neither decision suggests that Indian nations are sovereign in the strictest sense of the word. In the 1832 decision, Marshall opined that Indian nations are "distinct, independent political communities" and therefore could not be subjected to the laws of the state in which they lie. Accordingly, Indian tribes are sovereign vis-à-vis other state and local governments but not vis-à-vis the federal government.

With the debate centering on which governments are sovereign, almost no attention has been given to the derivation of tribal authority and the basis of its sovereignty vis-à-vis individual tribal members. Since Marshall's opinions specifically applied to one of the "Five Civilized Tribes," the issue of tribal authority warranted less attention. The Cherokees had a formal legal code with well-developed government authority that specified the relationship between individual Indians and the tribe (see Debo, 1970, pp. 113–114). For the Plains Indians, however, tribal government generally had much less meaning at the time Indians were relegated to reservations. Nearly all the Plains Indians lived in relatively independent groups (usually families or clans) where individual freedom was paramount. When there was collective action for hunting or warfare, leaders acquired limited sovereign power for a limited time. To thrust upon an institutional environment grounded in the sovereignty of individuals and small groups the notion of a sovereign nation is putting the cart before the horse.

Before Indian tribes, especially those with a tradition of individualism, can establish their sovereignty, they must establish the nature of the relationship between individual Indians and tribal government. This was tried under the IRA, but the effort amounted to little more than superimposing an Anglo-American constitutional government on Indians. While the formality of written words was put into the constitutions, there was no real social contract. By and large, the constitutions adopted under the IRA did not link the informal customs and cultures of the various tribes with the formal constitutional rules.

If we begin by assuming "individual sovereignty and show how various organizations and collectivities might be built from individual choices" (Roback, 1992, p. 6), we are more likely to understand how sovereign individuals relate to a sovereign nation and how sovereign nations relate to one another. In the case of many Indian tribes, this relationship was developed for warfare, the main margin on which most Indian interaction with either other Indians or whites took place in the late nineteenth century. War chiefs were in a position to make treaties with the United States as leaders of their respective sovereign nations, but the fact that they had little control over their subjects once the treaty was signed indicates that the rules governing the collectivity known as a sovereign nation did not extend much beyond warfare. Yet the interaction between Indian nations placed on reservations and other governmental units required collective action if the Indian nations were to retain any sovereignty.

To develop collective sovereignty, Indians will have to return to the basics of individual sovereignty and build from the ground up. In Roback's words, this approach is "profoundly individualistic" (1992, p. 6) and therefore may seem inimical to the accepted mind set of Indians as communal societies. However, assuming that a particular set of communal institutions should govern individual relationships is, once again, imposing a set of rules from the top down. In contrast, self-determination begins with the individual, as it did prior to European contact, and builds to collective action. Some tribes, such as the Cochiti, Mescalero Apache, and the Flathead, seem to have developed social contracts wherein the formal institutions that govern collective action jibe with the informal customs and culture (see Cornell & Kalt, 1992a). Interestingly, these three cases rely on very different structures for limiting the sovereign powers of the tribal government: benevolent theocracy, strong chief executive, and parliamentary, respectively. What appears important is that each structure works because it fits into the broader social context. Other tribes, most notably the Crow, which is quintessentially democratic, have made little institutional or economic progress because their tribal structure has no checks and balances; individuals, clans, and families are able to exploit the power of the sovereign nation for their own benefit. As one tribal member put it, the Crow tribal structure with its possibilities for patronage allows the individual "to get as much out of the tribe as possible" (quoted in Lopach, Brown, & Clow, 1990, p. 61). Tribal sovereignty in this setting is destined to promote institutional instability and economic stagnation. The Crow tribe recently tried to revise its constitution with little success because it contained "too much change in too short of a time" (Lorna Thackery cited in Lopach, Brown, & Clow, 1990, p. 74). Nonetheless, the effort to reconsider the relationship between the sovereign tribe and sovereign individuals is precisely what must occur if Indians are to find an institutional mix that promotes self-determination and economic progress.

Lesson 5: Binding the Sovereign Is the Ultimate Problem[2]

The fundamental problem facing any nation is how to provide the sovereign government with enough authority and power to do those things that enhance freedom and economic productivity without that power being used to transfer wealth from other citizens to those with power.[3] Indian nations are no exception. Granting the sovereign power to make unilateral decisions is necessary for at least two reasons. First, a sovereign government can exercise its power to enforce individual rights against takings by other individuals, by collective groups under the sovereign's authority, and by other sovereigns. This is the protective role for government. Second, sovereign power is necessary to produce certain public goods that might not otherwise be forthcoming. Sovereign governments have both a protective and productive role to play in any society, but this role requires coercive authority on the part of the government, making the ultimate problem one of limiting the use of that authority.

In establishing a sovereign government, citizens must recognize the potential that the powers necessary for protective and productive roles can be diverted toward transfer activity. For example, suppose that agents for the sovereign government use the sovereign powers to tax one group of citizens to provide wealth for another group. In such a world, the incentive to produce wealth will surely be diminished as individuals devote their efforts to defending their wealth against transfers or to convincing the government to transfer wealth in their direction.[4]

Consider the potential for using the justice system to transfer wealth. Suppose a company enters into an agreement with a sovereign nation to build a production facility that will employ citizens of the nation, and the sovereign nation in return agrees to lower taxes and limit regulations. After the investment has been made by the company, the investment can be held hostage by the sovereign who can take unilateral coercive actions. In this situation, what recourse will the company have if the nation reneges on its promise?

The standard response is that the harmed party can take the case to court for adjudication, but two factors make this response problematic when dealing with a sovereign. First, there is the possibility that the court that derives its authority from the sovereign will side with the sovereign. Second, even if the court finds the sovereign in violation of the agreement, there is, by definition of sovereignty, no authority to coerce the sovereign nation into abiding by the contract. "The exercise of sovereign powers in this way diminishes gains from trade as potential associates shy away from agreements" and therefore raises a paradox: *"Ceteris paribus*, the greater the sovereign's ability to impel submission by citizens, the less the ability of a third-party arbiter to compel performance by the sovereign, and so the less the sovereign's ability to induce voluntary cooperation. This paradox turns the sovereign's power into the sovereign's handicap" (Haddock, 1994, p. 130).

This paradox will be worse for sovereign nations that have not had an opportunity to establish a reputation for abiding by contracts or for those that may not be around long enough to care about their reputation. Comparing the United States with emerging eastern European countries, for example, it is likely that potential investors would find an agreement with the U.S. government more appealing. Not only is there a reputation for justice in the United States but there is a sense of longevity that increases the probability of collecting a return on investments.

There are two possibilities for mitigating the adverse effects of the paradox. One is to adopt and adhere to a constitution that specifies in a higher law how the sovereign must behave. Unfortunately, because constitutions are always subject to interpretation, there remains the question of who will interpret and enforce the higher rules. Haddock proposes that an alternative is for the sovereign to cede some of its powers "to another sovereign that is more likely to adhere to promises" (1994, p. 131).

Because of "American Indian reservations' small economic size, their legal immaturity, the uncertainty about the future of their status as sovereigns, and a chronic possibility of free-riding on other tribes' reputations" (Haddock, 1994, p. 131), they are particularly subject to the sovereign's paradox. Unfortunately, neither of the above options offers much hope for American Indian tribes to escape from the paradox. There are meaningful constitutional constraints for only a handful of tribes. To make matters worse, the U.S. Supreme Court ruled in *Merrion v. Jicarilla Apache Tribe* (455 U.S. 130 [1982])[5] that even though the tribe had entered into an explicit contract with an energy company not to raise taxes, the tribe's sovereign authority allowed it to renege on that contract by imposing a severance tax on oil and gas. The implications of this decision are far reaching.

[First] investors entering new relationships would adjust upwards the contractually stipulated returns they would require before commencing investment, on the expectation that some earnings ultimately will be taxed away. [Second] the increased potential for tribal opportunism also would divert investment funds from on-reservation projects to off-reservation ones. (Haddock, 1994, p. 137)

Subsequent rulings in *Southland Royalty Co. v. Navajo Tribe of Indians* (715 F. 2d 486 [10th Cin. 1983]) and *Kerr-McGee Corp. v. Navajo Tribe* (471 U.S. 195 [1985]) have further entrenched the tribes' powers to tax and regulate as sovereigns. Because these rulings open the door for tribal opportunism in dealings with potential investors, it is likely that some investors will chose not to deal with reservation economies.

The lesson from this sovereign's paradox is that Indian tribes must discover ways to bind themselves in contractual arrangements. Increasing the authority of tribal courts may extend sovereignty, but in light of the Supreme Court's position this will not make potential investors feel more secure in their dealings with tribes. Establishing a reputation for adhering to contracts will help, but it will take time to overcome perceptions of tribal opportunism. To rise above the paradox, tribes must consider following Haddock's advice to cede some sovereignty to a mature sovereign with a reputation for administering justice, but

this requires the other's acquiescence. The smaller and more immature the sovereign, the more urgent that result. Yet ceding some sovereignty is impossible without the better-formed jurisdiction's cooperation. Recent United States' court decisions have not been helpful in that regard. The governmental sovereignty of American Indian reservations has been jealously defended, even enhanced, by the federal courts. If no credible judiciary will guarantee an Indian's word then who will? An inattentive, undiscriminating determination to retain and enhance every aspect of tribal sovereignty cannot improve the typical reservation Indian's economic prospects, although it may well improve the prospects of those tribal politicians who channel the benefits, and optimize over an abbreviated period. (1994, p. 141)

Ultimately, self-determination and tribal sovereignty will require constitutional limits on tribal opportunism and a higher authority with a reputation for enforcing those limits. Until sovereign tribal governments are able to bind themselves in ways that ensure returns on long-term investments, economic progress on reservations is likely to be elusive.

The Future

Reflecting on the history of Indian institutions, it is clear that indigenous people in North America demonstrated a remarkable ability to adapt. Necessity was no less the mother of invention for institutions than it was for technology, and Indians rose to the challenge of getting the incentives right in a variety of ways. Their institutional responses may not always have followed the prescriptions of modern private property, though private ownership was not alien to Indians, but they did rely on many informal rules that provided positive rewards and negative penalties for individuals who failed to play by the rules of the game.

The history of Indian-white relations is not as bleak as it is often presented. Early interaction like that at the Pilgrim's first Thanksgiving suggests that there were gains from trade. In retrospect, questions can be raised about the distribution of the gains, but the fact that there was voluntary interaction at local levels implies that both Indians and whites had an incentive to cooperate.

As interaction graduated from individual and small groups to the federal government, the bargaining power of Indians declined and coercion replaced voluntary interaction. The Indian Wars and reservation policies of the late nineteenth century epitomize the exercise of federal dominion over Indians, a dominion that continues today. The difference today is that instead of exerting military force, the federal government dominates the day-to-day management of Indian resources and controls transfer policies that keep Indians dependent on the federal bureaucracy.

On the brighter side of Indian-white relations is the fact that the U.S. government has recognized the sovereignty of Indian nations. This recognition of Indian sovereignty has laid the foundation for self-determination that can be exploited by Indian nations wanting to escape the trap of reservation status.

The future for Indians will depend on how well they can build on their sovereign foundation. It simply will not do to accept that Indian tribes survived because of their reverence for social and natural environments. Contrary to popular myth, Indians were no more or less individualistic than other societies. Individual freedom was a hallmark of most Indian tribes, but they did know how and where to use collective action to achieve protective and productive ends. Rather than being communal by nature, they chose to subject individual behavior to collective authority determined and constrained by religion, ritual, and informal customs and norms. Instead of relying on myths that Indians were able to set aside self-interest and live in harmony with one another and with nature, the search for self-determination will be better served if Indians and non-Indians alike learn from the rich institutional history of North America's first inhabitants.

Notes

1. Such results, mirrored in *Property Rights and Indian Economies* (Anderson 1992), led Trosper to the conclusion that "in spite of the failures of the allotment policy and termination, proponents of private property systems continue their efforts" (1992, p. 322, fn. 28). Indeed, it is important to continue efforts to understand private property systems as they relate to Indian history and to present reservation productivity. Once this understanding exists, it is up to each tribe to decide what incentives systems it wants to adopt.

2. This section borrows heavily from the insights in Haddock (1994).

3. North, Anderson, and Hill (1983, ch. 2) discuss the protective, productive, and predatory roles of the state in more detail.

4. For a more complete discussion of the impacts of transfer activity, see Anderson and Hill (1980).

5. For a more complete discussion of this and other cases involving Indian sovereignty, see Haddock (1994).

REFERENCES

Albers, Patricia C. 1993. "Symbiosis, Merger, and War: Contrasting Forms of Intertribal Relationship Among Historic Plains Indians," in *The Political Economy of North American Indians*, John H. Moore, ed. Norman: University of Oklahoma Press.

Alchian, Armen A. 1950. "Uncertainty, Evolution and Economic Theory," *Journal of Political Economy* 58 (3): 211–221.

——— and Harold Demsetz. 1972. "Production, Information Costs, and Efficiency," *American Economic Review* 62 (5): 777–795.

Alston, Lee J. and Pablo T. Spiller. 1992. "A Congressional Theory of Indian Property Rights: The Cherokee Outlet," in *Property Rights and Indian Economies*, Terry L. Anderson, ed. Lanham, MD: Rowman and Littlefield.

Anderson, Terry L., ed. 1992. *Property Rights and Indian Economies*. Lanham, MD: Rowman and Littlefield.

Anderson, Terry L. and P. J. Hill. 1975. "The Evolution of Property Rights: A Study of the American West," *Journal of Law and Economics* 18 (1): 163–179.

———. 1980. *The Birth of a Transfer Society*. Stanford, CA: Hoover Institution Press.

———. 1983. "Privatizing the Commons: An Improvement?" *Southern Economic Journal* 50 (2): 438–450.

———. 1991. "The Race for Property Rights," *Journal of Law and Economics* 33 (April): 177–197.

Anderson, Terry L. and Dean Lueck. 1992a. "Agricultural Development and Land Tenure in Indian Country," in *Property Rights and Indian Economies*, Terry L. Anderson, ed. Lanham, MD: Rowman and Littlefield.

———. 1992b. "Land Tenure and Agricultural Productivity on Indian Reservations," *Journal of Law and Economics* 35: 427–454.

Anderson, Terry L. and Fred S. McChesney. 1994. "Raid or Trade: An Economic Model of Indian White Relations," *Journal of Law and Economics* 37 (April): 39–74.

Anderson, Terry L. and Randy Simmons, eds. 1993. *The Political Economy of Customs and Culture: Informal Solutions to the Commons Problem*. Lanham, MD: Rowman and Littlefield.

Arthur, George W. 1975. "An Introduction to the Ecology of Early Historic Communal Bison Hunting Among the Northern Plains Indians." National Museum of Man Mercury Series, Archeological Survey of Canada, Paper No. 37. Ottawa: National Museums of Canada.

Axtell, James. 1988. "Through Another Glass Darkly: Early Indian Views of Europeans," in *After Columbus: Essays in the Ethnohistory of Colonial North America*. New York: Oxford University Press.

Baden, John, Richard Stroup, and Walter A. Thurman. 1981. "Myths, Admonitions, and Rationality: The American Indian as a Resource Manager," *Economic Inquiry* 19 (1): 132–143.

Bailey, Martin J. 1992. "Approximate Optimality of Aboriginal Property Rights," *Journal of Law and Economics* 35 (April): 183–198.

Barreiro, Jose, ed. 1988. *Indian Roots of American Democracy*. Ithaca, NY: American Indian Program, Cornell University.

Barsh, Russel L. 1977. *The Washington Fishing Rights Controversy: An Economic Critique*. Seattle: University of Washington Graduate School of Business Administration.

———. 1987. "Plains Indian Agrarianism and Class Conflict," *Great Plains Quarterly* 7 (Spring): 83–90.

Barsh, Russel and Katherine Diaz-Knauf. 1984. "The Structure of Federal Aid for Indian Programs in the Decade of Prosperity, 1970–1980," *American Indian Quarterly* 8 (1): 1–29.

Barsness, Larry. 1985. *Heads, Hides, and Horns*. Fort Worth: Texas Christian University Press.

Basso, Keith H. 1970. *The Cibecue Apache*. New York: Holt, Rinehart and Winston.

Bates, Robert H. 1989. *Beyond the Miracle of the Market: The Political Economy of Agrarian Development in Kenya*. Cambridge: Cambridge University Press.

Bennett, John W. 1989. "Human Adaptations to the North American Great Plains and Similar Environments," in *The Struggle for the Land*, Paul A. Olson, ed. Lincoln: University of Nebraska Press.

Benson, Bruce. 1989. *The Enterprise of Law: Justice without the State*. San Francisco: Pacific Research Institute.

Benson, Bruce. 1992. "Customary Indian Law: Two Case Studies," in *Property Rights and Indian Economies*, Terry L. Anderson, ed. Lanham, MD: Rowman and Littlefield.

Beers, Henry P. 1975. *The Military Frontier 1815-46*. Philadelphia: Porcupine Press.

Black, Henry C. 1983. *Black's Law Dictionary*, abridged 5th edition. St. Paul: West.

Branch, E. Douglas. 1962. *The Hunting of Buffalo*. Lincoln: University of Nebraska Press.

Brasser, Ted J. 1974. "Riding on the Frontier's Crest: Machican Indian Culture and Culture Change." Ethnology Division. Paper No. 13. Ottawa: National Museums of Canada.

Bromley, Daniel W., ed. 1992. *Making the Commons Work*. San Francisco: Institute for Contemporary Studies.

Brown, Dee. 1970. *Bury My Heart at Wounded Knee*. New York: Holt, Rinehart and Winston.

Carlson, Leonard A. 1981. *Indians, Bureaucrats, and the Land: The Dawes Act and the Decline of Indian Farming*. Westport, CT: Greenwood Press.

————. 1992. "Learning to Farm: Indian Land Tenure and Farming Before the Dawes Act," in *Property Rights and Indian Economies*, Terry L. Anderson, ed. Lanham, MD: Rowman and Littlefield.

Catlin, George. 1965 [1841]. *Letters and Notes on the Manners, Customs, and Conditions of the North American Indians*, 2 vols. Reprint. Minneapolis: Ross and Haines.

Champagne, Duane. 1992. "Economic Culture, Institutional Order, and Sustained Market Enterprise: Comparisons of Historical and Contemporary American Indian Cases," in *Property Rights and Indian Economies*, Terry L. Anderson, ed. Lanham, MD: Rowman and Littlefield.

Chapel, Charles Edward. 1961. *Guns of the Old West*. New York: Coward-McCann.

Chase, Alston. 1986. *Playing God in Yellowstone*. Boston: Atlantic Monthly Press.

Cheung, Steven N.S. 1983. "The Contractual Nature of the Firm," *Journal of Law and Economics* 26 (1): 1–21.

Clark, A. McFadyen. 1981. "Koyukon," *Handbook of North American Indians—Subarctic*, vol. 6. Washington, DC: Smithsonian Institution.

Coase, Ronald. 1937. "The Nature of the Firm," *Economica* 4: 386–405.

Cohen, Felix. 1947. "Original Indian Title," *Minnesota Law Review* 32: 28–59.

Commissioner of Indian Affairs. 1887. *Annual Reports*. Washington, DC: U.S. Government Printing Office.

———. 1951. *Annual Reports*. Washington, DC: U.S. Government Printing Office.

Connell, Evan S. 1988. *Cavalier in Buckskin*. Norman: University of Oklahoma Press.

Cooter, Robert D. and Daniel L. Rubinfield. 1989. "Economic Analysis of Legal Disputes and Their Resolution," *Journal of Economic Literature* 27: 1067–1097.

Copper, John M. 1949. "Indian Land Tenure Systems," in *Indians of the United States*. (Contributions by Members of the Delegation, and by Advisers to the Policy Board of the National Indian Institute, for the Second Inter-American Conference on Indian Life, Cuzco, Peru.)

Cornell, Stephen and Joseph A. Kalt. 1991. "Where's the Glue? Institutional Bases of American Indian Economic Development," *Malcolm Wiener Center for Social Policy Working Paper Series*, H-91-2. John F. Kennedy School of Government, Harvard University. March.

———. 1992a. "Culture and Institutions as Public Goods: American Indian Economic Development as a Problem of Collective Action," in *Property Rights and Indian Economies*, Terry L. Anderson, ed. Lanham, MD: Rowman and Littlefield.

———. 1992b. *What Can Tribes Do? Strategies and Institutions in*

American Indian Economic Development. Los Angeles: University of California American Indian Studies Center.

Dalton, George. 1961. "Economic Theory and Primitive Society," *American Anthropologist* 63 (1): 1–25.

Dawkins, Richard. 1976. *The Selfish Gene.* New York: Oxford University Press.

Debo, Angie. 1970. *A History of the Indians of the United States.* Norman: University of Oklahoma Press.

Deloria, Vine, Jr., ed. 1985. *American Indian Policy in the Twentieth Century.* Norman: Oklahoma University Press.

———— and Clifford M. Lytle. 1984. *The Nations Within: The Past and Future of American Indian Sovereignty.* New York: Pantheon Books.

Demsetz, Harold. 1967. "Toward a Theory of Property Rights," *American Economic Review* 57 (2): 347–359.

Denig, Edwin T. 1930. "Indian Tribes of the Upper Missouri," in *46th Annual Report* (1928–29), Bureau of American Ethnology, J. N. B. Hewitt, ed. Washington, DC: U.S. Government Printing Office.

Dorner, Peter P. 1961. "Needed: A New Policy for American Indians," *Land Economics* 37: 162–173.

Eggertsson, Thráinn. 1990. *Economic Behavior and Institutions.* New York: Cambridge University Press.

Ellickson, Robert C. 1991. *Order Without Law: How Neighbors Settle Disputes.* Cambridge, MA: Harvard University Press.

Ellis, Florence Hawley. 1979. "Isleta Pueblo," *Handbook of North American Indians*, vol. 9. Washington, DC: Smithsonian Institution.

Ewers, John C. 1958. *The Blackfeet: Raiders on the Northwestern Plains.* Norman: University of Oklahoma Press.

————. 1969. *The Horse in Blackfoot Indian Culture.* Washington, DC: Smithsonian Institution Press.

————. 1968. *Indian Life on the Upper Missouri.* Norman: University of Oklahoma Press.

Faegre, Torvald. 1979. *Tents: Architecture of the Nomads.* Garden City, NY: Anchor Press/Doubleday.

Farb, Peter. 1968. *Man's Rise to Civilization as Shown by the Indians of North America.* New York: Dutton.

Farnham, Thomas J. 1843. *Travels in the Great Western Prairies, the*

Anahuac and Rocky Mountains, and in the Oregon Territory. New York: Greeley and McElrath.

Forde, C. Daryll. 1931. "Hopi Agriculture and Land Ownership," _The Journal of the Royal Anthropological Institute of Great Britain and Ireland_ 61: 357–405.

Fowler, Catherine S. 1986. _Handbook of North American Indians— Great Basin_, vol 11. Washington, DC: Smithsonian Institution.

Freed, Stanley A. 1960. "Changing Washo Kinship," _Anthropological Records_ 14 (6): 349–418.

Getches, David H. and Charles F. Wilkinson. 1986. _Federal Indian Law_, 2nd edition. St. Paul, MN: West.

Goldsmidt, Walter. 1951. "Ethics and the Structure of Society: An Ethnological Contribution to the Sociology of Knowledge," _American Anthropologist_ 53: 506–524.

Grinnell, George Bird. 1962. _Blackfoot Lodge Tales_. Lincoln: University of Nebraska Press.

———. 1972. _The Cheyenne Indians, Their History and Ways of Life_, vol. 1. Lincoln: University of Nebraska Press.

Haddock, David D. 1994. "Foreseeing Confiscation by the Sovereign: Lessons from the American West," in _The Political Economy of the American West_, Terry L. Anderson and Peter J. Hill, eds. Lanham, MD: Rowman and Littlefield.

Hames, Raymond. 1987. "Game Conservation or Efficient Hunting," in _The Question of the Commons_, Bonnie M. McCay and James M. Acheson, eds. Tucson: University of Arizona Press.

Hardin, Garrett. 1968. "The Tragedy of the Commons," _Science_ 162: 1243–1248.

Henry, Alexander and David Thompson. 1965. _New Light on the Early History of the Greater Northwest: The Manuscripts and Journals of Alexander Henry and David Thompson, 1799–1814_, Elliott Coues, ed. 3 vols. in 2. Minneapolis: Ross and Haines.

Higgs, Robert. 1982. "Legally Induced Technical Regress in the Washington Salmon Fishery," _Research in Economic History_ 7: 55–86.

Hoebel, E. Adamson. 1954. _The Law of Primitive Man_. Cambridge, MA: Harvard University Press.

Holm, Tom. 1985. "The Crisis in Tribal Government," in _American Indian Policy in the Twentieth Century_, Vine Deloria, Jr., ed. Norman: University of Oklahoma Press.

Hornaday, William T. 1889. "The Extermination of the American Bison, with a Sketch of Its Discovery and Life History." _Report_ *of the U.S. National Museum, 1887* (Part 2, 367–548). Washington, DC: U.S. Government Printing Office.

Hosley, Edward H. 1981. "Kolchan," *Handbook of North American Indians—Subarctic*, vol. 6. Washington, DC: Smithsonian Institution.

Hughes, Jonathan R. T. 1976. *Social Control in the Colonial Economy*. Charlottesville: University of North Carolina Press.

Huffman, James L. 1992. "An Exploratory Essay on Native Americans and Environmentalism," *University of Colorado Law Review* 63 (4): 901–920.

Hurt, F. Douglas. 1987. *Indian Agriculture in America: Prehistory to the Present*. Lawrence: University of Kansas Press.

Jefferson, Thomas. 1955. *Notes on the State of Virginia (1787)*, William Peden, ed. Chapel Hill: University of North Carolina Press.

Johnsen, D. Bruce. 1986. "The Formation and Protection of Property Rights Among the Southern Kwakiutl Indians," *Journal of Legal Studies* 15: 41–68.

Josephy, Alvin M., Jr. 1968. *The Indian Heritage of America*. New York: Bantam Books.

Juergensmayer, J. C. and J. B. Wadley. 1974. "The Common Lands Concept: A 'Commons' Solution to a Common Environmental Problem," *Natural Resources Journal* 14 (3): 361–381.

Kappler, Charles J., ed. 1904. *Indian Affairs: Laws and Treaties*, 7 vols. Washington, DC: U.S. Government Printing Office.

Karpoff, Jonathan M. and Edward M. Rice. 1989. "Organizational Form, Share Transferability, and Firm Performance: Evidence from the ANCSA Corporations," *Journal of Financial Economics* 24 (1): 69–105.

Kennard, Edward A. 1979. "Hopi Economy and Subsistence," *Handbook of North American Indians*, vol. 9. Washington, DC: Smithsonian Institution.

Kickingbird, Kirke and Karen Ducheneaux. 1973. *One Hundred Million Acres*. New York: Macmillan.

Krepps, Matthew B. 1992. "Can Tribes Manage Their Own Resources? The 638 Program and American Indian Forestry," in *What Can Tribes Do?*, Stephen Cornell and Joseph A. Kalt, eds. Los Angeles: University of California American Indian Studies Center.

Larpenteur, Charles. 1898. *Forty Years a Fur Trader on the Upper*

Missouri: The Personal Narrative of Charles, Larpenteur, vol. 2, Elliott Coues, ed. New York: F. P. Harper.

Levitan, Sar A. and William B. Johnston. 1975. _Indian Giving: Federal Programs for Native Americans_. Baltimore: Johns Hopkins University Press.

Lewis, Lloyd. 1950. _Captain Sam Grant_. Boston: Little Brown.

Linton, Ralph M. 1942. "Land Tenure in Aboriginal America," in _The Changing Indian_, Oliver LaFarge, ed. Norman: University of Oklahoma Press.

Libecap, Gary D. and Ronald N. Johnson. 1980. "Legislating Commons: The Navaho Tribal Council and the Navaho Range," _Economic Inquiry_ 18: 69–86.

Lopach, James, Margery Hunter Brown, and Richmond L. Clow. 1990. _Tribal Government Today: Politics on Montana Indian Reservations_. Boulder, CO: Westview Press.

Lowie, Robert H. 1920. _Primitive Society_. New York: Boni and Liveright.

———. 1935. _The Crow Indians_. New York: Farrar and Rinehart.

———. 1940. "Ethnographic Notes on the Washo," _American Archaeology and Ethnology_ 36: 301–351.

———. 1982. _Indians of the Plains_. Lincoln: University of Nebraska Press.

Lueck, Dean. 1993. "Contracting Into the Commons," in _The Political Economy of Customs and Culture: Informal Solutions to the Commons Problem_, Terry L. Anderson and Randy T. Simmons, eds. Lanham, MD: Rowman and Littlefield.

Matheson, David. 1992. "Economic Development—The Challenge of the 1990s," unpublished luncheon address delivered to the 1992 Reservation Economic Summit, Seattle, WA, May 11.

McChesney, Fred S. 1992. "Government as Definer of Property Rights: Indian Lands, Ethnic Externalities, and Bureaucratic Budgets," in _Property Rights and Indian Economies_, Terry L. Anderson, ed. Lanham, MD: Rowman and Littlefield.

McNeill, William H. 1963. _The Rise of the West_. Chicago: University of Chicago Press.

Medicine Crow, Joe. 1978. "Notes on Crow Indian Buffalo Jump Traditions," _Plains Anthropologist_ 23 (82, Part 2): 249–253.

Mulloy, William. 1958. A Preliminary Historical Outline for the Northwestern Plains. _University of Wyoming Publications_ 22 (1).

National Congress on American Indians. 1968. *Heirship: A Short Report*. Denver: National Congress on American Indians.

Netboy, Anthony. 1958. *Salmon of the Pacific Northwest: Fish vs. Dams*. Portland, OR: Binfords and Mort.

North, Douglass C. 1990. *Institutions, Institutional Change and Economic Performance*. Cambridge: Cambridge University Press.

North, Douglass C., Terry L. Anderson, and Peter J. Hill. 1983. *Growth and Welfare in the American Past*. Englewood Cliffs, NJ: Prentice Hall.

Olson, Paul A., ed. 1989. *The Struggle for the Land: Indigenous Insight and Industrial Empire in the Semiarid World*. Lincoln: University of Nebraska Press.

Ostrum, Elinor. 1990. *Governing the Commons: The Evolution of Institutions for Collective Actions*. Cambridge: Cambridge University Press.

Otis, Delos Sacket. 1973. *The Dawes Act and the Allotment of Indian Lands*, Francis Paul Prucha, ed. Norman: University of Oklahoma Press.

Philip, Kenneth R. 1977. *John Collier's Crusade for Indian Reform 1920–1954*. Tucson: University of Arizona Press.

———, ed. 1986. *Indian Self-Rule: First-Hand Accounts of Indian-White Relations from Roosevelt to Reagan*. Salt Lake City: Howe Brothers.

Posner, Richard A. 1980. "A Theory of Primitive Society, with Special Reference to Primitive Law," *Journal of Law and Economics* 23 (1): 1-54.

Provinse, John H. 1955. "The Underlying Sanctions of Plains Indian Culture," in *Social Anthropology of North American Tribes*, Fred Eggan, ed. Chicago: University of Chicago Press.

Prucha, Francis Paul. 1962. *American Indian Policy in the Formative Years: The Indian Trade and Intercourse Acts, 1790–1834*. Cambridge: Harvard University Press.

———. 1973. *Americanizing the American Indian*. Cambridge: Harvard University Press.

———. 1984. *The Great Father: The United States Government and the American Indians*. Lincoln: University of Nebraska Press.

Roback, Jennifer. 1992. "Exchange, Sovereignty, and Indian-Anglo Relations," in *Property Rights and Indian Economies*, Terry L. Anderson, ed. Lanham, MD: Rowman and Littlefield.

Rogers, Edward S. and Eleanor Leacock. 1981. "Montagnais-

Naskapi," _Handbook of North American Indians—Subarctic_, vol. 6. Washington, DC: Smithsonian Institution.

Rogers, Edward S. and J. Garth Taylor. 1981. "Northern Ojibwa," _Handbook of North American Indians—Subarctic_, vol. 6. Washington, DC: Smithsonian Institution.

Royal, Robert. 1992. "1492 and Multiculturalism," _The Intercollegiate Review_ 27 (Spring): 3–10.

Russell, Don. 1973. "How Many Indians Were Killed?" _American West_, 10 (4): 42–47.

Sass, H. R. 1936. "Hoofs on the Prairie," _Country Gentleman_, July.

Schemeckebier, Laurence R. 1927. _The Office of Indian Affairs_. Baltimore: Johns Hopkins Press.

Schultz, James Willard. 1907. _My Life As an Indian: The Story of a Red Woman and a White Man in the Lodges of the Blackfeet_. Boston: Houghton Mifflin.

Shimkin, Demitri B. 1986. "Eastern Shoshone," _Handbook of North American Indians_, vol. 11: 308–335. Washington, DC: Smithsonian Institution.

Smith, Rodney T. 1992. "Water Rights Claims in Indian Country," in _Property Rights and Indian Economies_, Terry L. Anderson, ed. Lanham, MD: Rowman and Littlefield.

Sorkin, Alan L. 1971. _American Indians and Federal Aid_. Washington, DC: Brookings Institution.

Speck, Frank G. 1939. "Aboriginal Conservators," _Bird Lore_ 40: 258–261.

Speck, Frank G. and Wendell S. Hadlock. 1946. "A Report on Tribal Boundaries and Hunting Areas of the Malecite Indians of New Brunswick," _American Anthropologist_ 48 (3): 355–374.

Steward, Julian H. 1934. "Ethnography of the Owens Valley Paiute," _American Archaeology and Ethnology_ 33 (1): 233–324.

———. 1938. _Basin-Plateau Aboriginal Sociopolitical Groups_. Smithsonian Institution, Bureau of American Ethnology, Bulletin 120. Washington, DC: U.S. Government Printing Office.

———. 1941. "Cultural Element Distributions: XIII Nevada Shoshoni," _Anthropological Records_ 4 (2): 209–259.

Stewart, Omer C. 1941. "Culture Element Distributions: XIV Northern Paiute," _Anthropological Records_ 4 (3): 361–446.

Stuart, Paul. 1987. _Nations Within Nations: Historical Statistics of American Indians_. New York: Greenwood Press.

Taylor, Theodore W. 1959. "The Regional Organization of the Bureau of Indian Affairs," Ph.D. dissertation, Harvard University, December.

———. 1984. *The Bureau of Indian Affairs*. Boulder, CO: Westview Press.

Timmons, Boyce D. 1980. "Foreword" in *The Peace Chiefs of the Cheyennes*, Stan Hoig, ed. Norman: University of Oklahoma Press.

Trenholm, Virginia Cole and Maurine Carley. 1964. *The Shoshonis, Sentinels of the Rockies*. Norman: University of Oklahoma Press.

Trosper, Ronald L. 1978. "American Indian Relative Ranching Efficiency." *American Economic Review* 68 (4): 503–516.

———. 1992. "Mind Sets and Economic Development on Indian Reservations," in *What Can Tribes Do?* Stephen Cornell and Joseph P. Kalt, eds. Los Angeles: University of California American Indian Studies Center.

Umbeck, John. 1981. "Might Makes Rights: A Theory of the Formation and Initial Distribution of Property Rights," *Economic Inquiry* 19 (1): 38–59.

U.S. Bureau of Indian Affairs. 1969. "Economic Development of Indian Communities." In *Toward Economic Development for Native American Communities*, Joint Economic Committee, U.S. Congress. Washington, DC: U.S. Government Printing Office.

U.S. Bureau of the Census. 1900. *Twelfth Census of the United States, 1900*, Vol. 5, *Agriculture*. Washington, DC: U.S. Government Printing Office.

———. 1975. *Historical Statistics of the United States, Colonial Times to 1970,* Bicentennial edition. Washington DC: U.S. Government Printing Office.

———. 1986. *Census of the Population, 1980. Subject Report: American Indians, Eskimos, and Aleuts on Identified Reservations and in the Historic Areas of Oklahoma (excluding urbanized areas)*. Washington, DC: U.S. Government Printing Office.

———. 1989. *1987 Census of Agriculture: State Advance Reports*, various states. Washington, DC: U.S. Government Printing Office.

U.S. Department of Agriculture, Soil Conservation Service. 1970. *Conservation Needs Inventory,* various states. Washington DC: U.S. Government Printing Office.

U.S. Department of the Interior. 1981. *Budget Justification, Fiscal Year 1981*. Washington DC: U.S. Government Printing Office.

———. 1986. *Report of the Task Force on Indian Economic Develop-ment*. Washington DC: U.S. Government Printing Office, July.

———, Bureau of Indian Affairs. 1987. *Natural Resources Informa-tion System*. Washington, DC: U.S. Government Printing Office.

U.S. House of Representatives. 1944. Select Committee on Indian Affairs, Report 2091, pursuant to H.R. 155, 2, 78th Cong., 2d sess., Washington, DC, December 23.

———. 1960. Committee on Interior and Insular Affairs. *Indian Heirship Land Study*. Pts. 1 and 2. 86th Cong., 2d sess. Wash-ington, DC: U.S. Government Printing Office.

U.S. Senate. 1943. Committee on Indian Affairs, Report 310, 78th Cong., 1st sess., June 11.

Usher, Peter J. 1992. "Property as the Basis of Inuit Hunting Rights," in *Property Rights and Indian Economies*, Terry L. Anderson, ed. Lanham, MD: Rowman and Littlefield.

Utley, Robert M. 1967. *Frontiersmen in Blue: The United States Army and the Indian, 1848–1865*. Lincoln: University of Nebraska Press.

———. 1984. *The Indian Frontier of the America West 1846–1890*. Albuquerque: New Mexico Press.

Washburn, Wilcomb E. 1971. *Red Man's Land/White Man's Law*. New York: Charles Scribner's Sons.

Webb, Walter Prescott. 1931. *The Great Plains*. New York: Grosset and Dunlap.

Wedel, Waldo R. 1941. "Environment and Native Subsistence Econo-mies in the Great Plains," *Smithsonian Miscellaneous Collec-tions* 101 (3): 1–29.

Wessel, Thomas R. 1976. "Agriculture, Indians, and American His-tory," *Agricultural History* 50 (1): 9–20.

White, Jon Manchip. 1979. *Everyday Life of North American Indians*. New York: Indian Head Books.

White, Richard. 1993. *It's Your Fortune and None of My Own*. Nor-man: University of Oklahoma Press.

Wilkinson, Charles F. 1987. *American Indians, Time, and the Law*. New Haven: Yale University Press.

Williams, Ethel J. 1970–71. "Too Little Land, Too Many Heirs—The Indian Heirship Land Problem," *Washington Law Review* 46: 709–744.

Wilson, Paul S. 1992. "What Chief Seattle Said," *Environmental Law* 22: 1451–1468.

Wishart, David J. 1990. "Compensation for Dispossession: Payments to the Indians for Their Lands on the Central and Northern Great Plains in the 19th Century," *National Geographic Research* 6 (1): 94–109.

Wissler, Clark. 1910. "Material Culture of the Blackfoot Indians," *Anthropological Papers of the American Museum of Natural History* 5(1): 1–176.

————. 1966. *Indians of the United States*. New York: Doubleday.

Wolf, Eric. 1982. *Europe and the People Without History*. Berkeley, CA: University of California Press.

Wood, Scott Alan. 1992. "The Elasticity of Force: Determinants of Terms of Trade in American Indian Treaties." Unpublished Master's Thesis, Montana State University, Bozeman, MT.

Wyman, Walker D. 1945. *The Wild Horse of the West*. Lincoln: University of Nebraska Press.

Yandle, Bruce. 1993. "Bootleggers and Baptists—Environmentalists and Protectionists: Old Reasons for New Coalitions," in *NAFTA and the Environment*, Terry L. Anderson, ed. San Francisco: Pacific Research Institute.

I N D E X

access
    controlled, 36-38
    to Indian land under General Allotment Act, 94-98, 102-104
    rules limiting access to commons, 52-53

accountability
    in collective decision making, 11
    decision maker's need for, 162
    evidence for effect of, 133
    lack of, 154
    relation to cultural constraints, 11-12

action, collective
    factors indecision for, 51-52
    free-rider problem, 25, 52
    incentives in rules for, 41-43
    tribal government as model for, 139-145

agricultural methods
    Indian property rights related to, 31-36
    pre-land allotment reserva-

tion practices, 113-116

agricultural productivity
    comparison of fee simple and trust lands, 121-125
    comparison of reservation fee simple and trust land, 124-131
    under different forms of land tenure, 124-131
    with institutional politicization, 90
    on reservation lands, 19-20, 116-121
    under reservation land tenure institutions, 112-113

Alchian, Armen A., 7, 11, 48, 52

alienation
    of allotted land, 117, 120
    constraints on individual trust land, 122, 125
    prevention under Indian Reorganization Act (1934), 120
    tribal resources for, 123
    value of land with, 122

allotment. *See* General Allotment